T0149553

Charmed Divorce

A Positive Twist on the D-Word

101 THINGS TO DO WHEN GETTING DIVORCED

LEAH SCOTT & ROBIN SASSI

BALBOA.
PRESS

A DIVISION OF HAY HOUSE

Balboa Press books may be ordered through booksellers or by contacting:

Balboa Press
A Division of Hay House
1663 Liberty Drive
Bloomington, IN 47403
www.balboapress.com
1 (877) 407-4847

Because of the dynamic nature of the Internet, any web addresses or links contained in this book may have changed since publication and may no longer be valid. The views expressed in this work are solely those of the author and do not necessarily reflect the views of the publisher, and the publisher hereby disclaims any responsibility for them.

The author of this book does not dispense medical advice or prescribe the use of any technique as a form of treatment for physical, emotional, or medical problems without the advice of a physician, either directly or indirectly. The intent of the author is only to offer information of a general nature to help you in your quest for emotional and spiritual well-being. In the event you use any of the information in this book for yourself, which is your constitutional right, the author and the publisher assume no responsibility for your actions.

Any people depicted in stock imagery provided by Thinkstock are models, and such images are being used for illustrative purposes only. Certain stock imagery © Thinkstock.

Print information available on the last page.

ISBN: 978-1-5043-7402-6 (sc)
ISBN: 978-1-5043-7403-3 (hc)
ISBN: 978-1-5043-7413-2 (e)

Library of Congress Control Number: 2017901460

Balboa Press rev. date: 02/14/2017

TABLE OF CONTENTS

Chapter Five

INTRODUCTION

At one of our bi-weekly coffee dates, we were talking about all the crazy stuff we were encountering with our divorces. We shared stories of court dates, child custody issues, and all the insanity that surrounds a divorce. As we left the coffee shop, we looked at each other and said at the same moment, "*I feel it's our duty to warn others about what they're in for.*" We laughed, and both looked at each other and agreed, "*Yes, we must*" and that is how Charmed Divorce was born.

What is a Charmed Divorce? It's a divorce that focuses on the positive. It's a way to let go of the past and move forward with your life with grace, dignity, and a sense of humor. In this book, we are going to share our secrets to experiencing divorce the Charmed way. We are here to tell you that the dreaded "D" word does not have to be devastating. Divorce CAN happen in a positive way.

Divorce is a journey from being with another person to being independent. On the journey through divorce, the events can be joyful, scary, sad, funny, and downright unnerving. There are times when the sky is clear and times when you think the sun will never shine again. And yes, there will be many storms. It is important to view this process as a journey and not as a static, unchanging event. In fact, there will be many changes, and it's important to stay level headed through the many storms thrown your way. The storms will pass, and the sun will shine again.

Though we are friends and coauthors of this book, we are both on our separate journeys. Some of our experiences have been similar, and some have been different. We each had our moments of breakdowns when we helped each other through it. On the flipside, we've had great laughs, many at the expense of our exes. We share some of these experiences with you along with the lessons we have learned.

You will get your divorce over and done with as quickly and safely as possible. Whatever situation you're in, you will get through it. We are here to help you through your personal journey and get you to a new, better version of your fabulous self. It is now *your* journey to having a Charmed Divorce.

A Little About Us

We have both gone through changes as a result of our divorces. We've taken hits and become strong. We've gained confidence in ourselves and our beliefs. We learned that we could get through a divorce gracefully and with dignity. We even learned how to work the remote control.

In the past few years, one of us got an MBA, the other a law degree, and both of us received a first class education in divorce. As we were going on this journey, we discovered that keeping our minds, bodies, and spirits aligned played a crucial role in maintaining our sanity through the difficulties of divorce and recovery. We share these experiences with you to guide you, comfort you, and sometimes help you see the humor in it all.

We were both in marriages lasting over ten years. Divorce is difficult, especially with children. We both made every attempt to do what we could to save the marriage. In spite of our efforts, it was not enough. Divorce happens. There was hurt, sadness, and anger on both sides. We recognize that some relationships are not made to be forever. We felt it was important to share this information for those who may be contemplating divorce or similar situations. We are here to share our trials and tribulations throughout this process. You are not alone. Always remember: This too shall pass. You will get through this process and even find some things to laugh about. You will become a stronger, more confident person in the end.

This book is a reference guide. It will help you when you are having a bad day or when you are not sure how to manage aspects of your divorce. It will help remind you to take care of yourself. You can read it cover-to-cover, or skip to the sections that are relevant to you. The ultimate goal is to help you to get through a tough time of your life, to know that you have support, and show you that it can be done with a bit of grace, a bit of humor, and a lot of charm.

Society usually portrays divorce as a bad thing. We are writing this book to change that societal perception. It's difficult when divorce happens, but some things are not meant to last, and it's okay to let it go. A divorce can set a person free, cause them to grow, and challenge them to find happiness. This guide will help you move on with the next chapter of your life. We guarantee if you go into your divorce with the correct mindset, it will be one of the greatest chapters!

We do have one critical piece of advice to give you before you go any further:

GET
LAID

If you are going through a divorce, there is a high chance that you and your ex have not had sex in quite a while. You may have been living in a sexual desert for some time. Do you even remember what it is like to enjoy sex? How long has it been? Don't push it. When you are ready, you'll know. At that time, get out there and take care of yourself! The first time being with another person is definitely a different experience. It can be strange and scary. On the other hand, maybe you are ready to get out there with a vengeance. In any event, it is exciting.

We also know that some of you have not been living in a sexual desert during your marriage. Short version: you had sex with someone who was not your spouse while married. We don't judge. Regardless of the situation, once you file for divorce or separation, and live in a separate dwelling from your ex, it is time to enjoy your new life. What better way then to have some great sex? So go on, and **Get Laid**! You deserve the attention and pleasure.

At the end of each section of this book, we offer various notes and activities, along with a complete "To Do" list at the end of the book. For example, on "Get Laid," which we just discussed, Leah will offer some notes, followed by Robin, and then an activity:

Note from Leah...

I wasn't ready for this until I moved out. However, it did not take me long to get into the dating scene, and boy did I have fun with it! Literally, *Men* is the operative word!

I had a friend who was just separated and was down on herself. It made me sad because my friend is such a beautiful person inside and out. I decided I was going to take her out and get her laid! She wasn't too keen on the idea. However, she obliged, and we hit up a bar that evening with another friend. We had the greatest time just being out, dancing with lots of laughter.

She ended up meeting a guy that night and they are still dating. Her face lights up when she talks about him. Unfortunately, too often in marriage you lose the attraction to one another and are just good friends. You are now single. It is time to be attracted to someone, and have the butterfly feelings of being with a new person. This is why it is so important to get out there and have fun. It is time to get your light back.

Note from Robin...

Sex is different for everybody. The last thing I wanted after being in a long relationship was to get laid. I was not in "that place." I figured that I would be ready when I was ready. Don't feel pressured. Take your time. You're an adult and know yourself pretty well. Lord knows you are not a virgin anymore so when the time comes, you will too. When I was finally ready, it was good. I mean really, really good. And weird. But good. Ok, it was great. Really great.

Activity: Get laid. Seriously. You know what they say. "That person is cranky. They need to get laid!"

Don't worry. Not all the activities in this book will be so blunt as the one we just gave you.

Now that we have this very important subject out of the way, we hope you enjoy reading this as much as we enjoyed writing it. Enjoy your new life, stay strong, and keep a smile on your face. It helps! This is what we call a Charmed Divorce.

Leah & Robin

Chapter One

BODY, MIND, & SPIRIT

What do body, mind, and spirit have to do with divorce? Everything! Divorce is one of the hardest things you will ever go through in your life. It will beat you down, make you feel insecure, financially devastate you, and, for better or for worse, change your life in ways you cannot imagine. Now is a time of tearing down and building up. You will be stretched to your limits. You will find out who your friends really are and who is eager to kick you when you are down. If you think that everyone loves you and no one would possibly think anything bad about you, think again. By divorcing, you have guaranteed that at least one person in the world has it out for you.

Divorce is a time when you will experience growth. Growth is all a part of the Charmed Divorce. Remember when you were a teenager? It was a crazy time for growth. You may think since you are an adult that you are all done with growth. Wrong. Now that your marriage is over, you will experience growth in a whole new way, the Charmed Way. As it was when you were a teenager, growing can be exciting and painful at the same time.

Keep laughing. Hang on. The worst may be here, behind you, or yet to come. You are not alone. We are here for you!

Your Amazing Body

Self Care ~ Exercise ~ Sleep ~ Mindful Breathing

We start with the body because taking care of your physical self is easier to start with. How your body feels affects the way your mind operates and positive body conditioning is good for the soul. Working on yourself from the outside in is a way to feel good inside *and* out.

<u>Engage in Self Care</u>

Feel like taking a nap on a Saturday afternoon? Want to take off for the weekend? Spontaneous vacations might not have been as easy to do when you were married. It required coordinating your calendar with another person. Now that you are on your own do what makes you feel good.

It is easy to get depressed after finishing a relationship. You might have let yourself go a bit. You are an adult – if you don't take care of yourself, no one else will. It is time to put "you" first. Self-care means doing what makes you feel good, even if you are feeling lousy.

We knew a man who went through a severe break-up. As the marriage fell apart, he held himself together by putting together a solid self-care regimen. This involved going to the gym four times a week, eating well, drinking plenty of water, and 30-minutes of meditation each night. Even though his marriage was ending, he continued to engage in self-care every day. After three months, the divorce was still going on, but he was better able to handle the stress, and he felt good that he could keep himself together.

Dedicate an hour a day to self-care. Concentrate first on your body. You don't have to spend money. Take that time to exercise, or do your nails, or give yourself a facial. Then use another day to journal, read, or take a walk. Catch up with old friends and stay away from divorce talk when you do. Talk about your hobbies or talk about your new life instead.

Do that mani-pedi and enjoy every moment of it! If you want to pamper your body inexpensively, you can use online coupons or find a salon that does it for less. Don't skip out on the things you love, just find a way to have them in a way you can afford. If these small moments in life make you feel good, you will be able to handle your divorce better, because you feel better about yourself.

Note from Leah...

It takes a while to decompress from your old life. I still have moments where I realize *"Oh, I don't have to coordinate with another person to go for a walk on the beach or get my nails done."* Coordinating schedules was a common occurrence while in a relationship and co-parenting. Now I have free time. Make an effort to do such things. It's liberating to treat yourself well.

Note from Robin...

I went through a mid-life crisis early. This crisis happened while I was married and nowhere near divorce. One thing my dad said was, "You need to do something that makes you feel good, even if it means you have to put it on a credit card to do it. You have to do something for yourself."

Going through this experience was a valuable lesson for me. I had denied myself small pleasures to the point that life had no flavor. I felt like I was going through the motions of my day. There was no joy and no reward for my hard work. I was breaking.

I began to take time for myself even though the demands on me were great. I bought myself a few new things even though I felt I couldn't afford them. Taking care of myself released the pressure I felt and gave me a little bit of happiness. That little bit made me feel like life was worth living.

Activity: Make a list of the top things you want to do for yourself this week. Start marking them off as you treat yourself to as many as you can.

Exercise

Now is the perfect time to get into an exercise routine. You do not have to join a gym, and you do not have to get a personal trainer. An exercise routine can be as cheap as you want, or as expensive. The key is to begin and to make it a regular part of your life. Once those endorphins start running, you will find that dealing with your divorce is easier. You will also have the added benefit of looking really hot in case you run into your ex or the new person of your dreams.

Exercise can keep you positive. As your life is realigning itself, you can make do with a "little in the morning, little at night." Take ten minutes in the morning for a few simple yoga exercises. Too busy? Really? Exercising by talking on the phone with friends while you walk the neighborhood. Take another ten minutes at night to do a few simple exercises.

The hardest part of doing anything long-term is to be consistent. Rather than exercising for a certain amount of time every week, just try to get to it every day. It is better to build up a good habit rather than trying to get it all done at once. You will find that the amount of time you exercise each day will naturally extend over time.

Find an exercise that interests you. Go to Yoga, Pilates, or whatever it takes. There are so many programs out there that cater to the different interests of people. Maybe you are into cross-fit or boxing. Find your niche. See what resonates with you and think outside of the box. For example, exercising does not always have to involve a class. There are active social clubs that center around physical activities. You can join these for kickball, flag football, golf, and even bowling. These clubs are co-ed and also give you an opportunity to meet new people.

If you are in a financial pinch, there is always the road. Give it a pounding, even if that pounding is a gentle 30-minute walk. Take the stairs instead of the elevator. Do lunges on the way to other rooms in your house. Exercise can be free. A workout can be anywhere! Inside, outside, or while you are watching TV. You can find a ton of resources on the internet. Get to it!

Find what works for you. This is the Charmed Way to take care of yourself. Exercising can heal your mind and soul, and you feel great as a result! Did we mention you will end up with a fabulous looking body? What are you waiting for?

Note from Leah...

Exercise is one of my happy places. It helps keep my mind in check. It is essential to find what works for you to stick with it. I have gone through many exercise fads that I love *i.e. kickboxing, Barre, and Pilates.* Walking is my other favorite. I am fortunate to live by the beach, so I make it a habit, walking near it often. It's also calming for me to walk near the ocean.

Walking is also a great way to combine exercise and spend time with a friend. Get a fitness tracker and compete with a friend each week. It makes it fun, and the competition gets you walking and running. It is time to make your health a priority so find what resonates with you and involve your friends. Find your calming place.

My best friend who never liked working out in big gyms (or even small ones for that matter), recently found a new love for skateboarding while teaching her kids. She said it's the best workout yet, and she loves it. It is perfect for her because she couldn't stick with the other fitness routines long-term.

There are many ways to integrate exercise into your life without a corporate gym membership. Park your car in the farthest parking spot from the store. Walk to the furthest bathroom at work. Do lunges while watching your show or during commercials. Don't allow yourself to watch your show unless you are on the stationary bike or doing some form of exercise. You get the idea. There are all types of ways to sneak it into your daily routine. No excuses.

Note from Robin...

There was a time during my divorce where I had to let exercise go. It's ok. Don't bash yourself if there's a period when this is just impossible. But keep this task in your mind.

After about a year, it was time for me to go back to exercising regularly. I realized how much I missed the positive experience of exercise *and* the side effect of a great body. Restarting my exercise routine created other self-care habits that I had ignored. I started drinking more water, cutting down on sugar, and watching my diet. All I did was dedicate ten minutes at the gym. That was all it took. After a while, I was back to ballet and Pilates, dropped five pounds, and had glorious skin from all the water and stimulation.

Activity: List the five top exercises you have heard about that sparked your interest. Look for deals in your area and sign up. Find your favorite. Be excited to try something new. Did someone say pole dancing?

<u>Get Sleep</u>

Stress will happen. Emergencies will occur. Children will cry. The ex will lie. But, through all the chaos and uncertainty, sleep will help. Sleep will center you, re-energize you, and clear your head. In an ideal world, we would have all of the benefits of sleep without having to put in the time. However, sacrificing sleep to get other things done is counter-productive. If you deny yourself sleep, you will find yourself less productive, and it is during this time in your life that there will be more demands on you than ever. Although the temptation to cut back on sleep will be there, remember that it simply is not worth it.

A woman we met told us that the secret to getting through her divorce was sleep. Whenever she felt overwhelmed, she took a nap or went to bed early that night. She said that her mind would work on the problem for her while she was sleeping and the next morning, she would always have a better perspective on what was bothering her.

Most people know that sleep is good for the body. But it can also be an escape. If you are still in the house with your ex, going to sleep is a good way to avoid him or her. It is also good to "sleep on" important decisions. Even after you are divorced, there will be additional stress if you have children. It is the rule, not the exception, that custody battles and child support tussles will continue until your youngest child reaches adulthood. When you feel your blood boil from the nasty email you just received from your ex, take the evening to sleep on it.

If you are recently separated, but not divorced yet, the conflict will be part of your foreseeable future, especially if you are still in the same house with your ex. If you are in the midst of your divorce, you will need energy for court, children, work, and the amazing sex you are going to have. It's not a time to be sleep deprived. It's also a time in your life where the decisions you make will have a long-lasting effect on you and your children. Having a good nights sleep and being well rested will center you so that you can make better decisions.

Note from Leah...

A bedtime routine is necessary for good sleep. I have always been aware of this and have always loved my sleep and bedtime. Bedtime has been my favorite time of day for many years, for several reasons. I view it as my 'me' time. It is the time of day that I look forward to reading, watching a favorite television show, or cuddling. It's the time of day to wind down and recharge.

However, it is difficult to stay on schedule when you are a newly single parent, or even a parent for that matter.

It's another reason a good night's sleep is crucial. I have a set bedtime every night I try to stick with it. I realize how quickly my body reacts when I do not. It is important to find the amount of sleep your body needs. Every person is different. Oh, and weekends don't count!

Note from Robin...

While getting divorced, there was a period where I was exhausted but couldn't sleep because of the stress. I would fall asleep at 10 PM then wake up several times during the night. My day was like a nightmare, and I was the walking dead, barely able to stand. I found that the lack of sleep was affecting my memory. I could not remember simple passwords to sites I visit every day. It was all I could do to shower, dress, and eat.

It took a while, but I eventually was able to get into a better sleep routine. I found sleep to be important in getting through my divorce. So many aspects of my life improved as a result. My mind was clear and I was able to focus on tasks so much better. I was less sensitive to criticism and was able to look at situations more logically.

Activity: Create a bedtime routine or download an app to help you get enough sleep. Sleep is a lot cheaper than a fancy eye cream.

<u>Practice Mindful Breathing</u>

How many times do we go through our day without taking the time to breathe? How many times do we forget to breathe when things get stressful? We hold our breath like we are stubborn children who do not get our way. We hold our breath like a person frozen in fear, afraid of harm. We hold our breath like we are sinking, drowning, and about to die.

This is why we need to breathe. It is essential during the stressful moments of divorce. We discuss meditation throughout this book. Mindful breathing is something to do throughout the entire day, not just during meditation. While meditation needs to take place in the right environment with no interruptions, breathing is an *act*, taking place all the time.

Some people use the phrase "one day at a time." Anyone going through the insanity of a divorce can tell you that a day can be too long. Even an hour can be too long. So shorten the time. How about trying "five minutes at a time"? During that five minutes, breathe. Exhale the negative and inhale the positive. If this means pulling over on the side of the freeway after a morning of divorce court, do it. If this means getting off the phone with your ex to recollect yourself, do it. Breathe.

Breathe in, breathe out. Again. Release.

You will become more conscious of your breathing habits when you practice mindful breathing. When those stressful moments hit you in the middle of the day, you can take the time to breathe in, breathe out, and release. If you only have to practice it once a day, you may be in a good place already. However, most people need to practice mindful breathing many times throughout their day. Take the time. Put a reminder on your phone to practice. Mindful breathing will soon become an automatic response to stress, and it will allow you to go through your divorce in a more positive way.

Note from Leah...

I have, time and again, defaulted to taking a deep breath to clear my head and tell myself "this too shall pass," and I promise, it will. Learn to breathe through the tough moments. This technique helps when you feel that you are about to break down in tears due to the overwhelming feeling of stress, or when you are getting ready to deal with a court hearing relating to your divorce. Whatever the stress may be, breathing will help. Just *breathe* through the moments.

Note from Robin...

This section is my favorite part of this book. Every time I read it, I am reminded to practice mindful breathing. Even as I read, I remember how important this is. I find myself breathing in-out, in-out.

There have been times where my breathing came in hysterical sobs. Sometimes I am truly centered and can breathe out my tension. Truth be told, I hate breathing. I just want to scream sometimes and let it all out. Then, I realize, "I'm breathing with volume!" Ha! Keep breathing!

Activity: Breathe with intent. Inhale deeply for four seconds. Hold your breath for four seconds, and exhale for four seconds. This really works for calming yourself down. Practice it. Remember 4-4-4.

Your Incredible Mind

Stay Positive ~ Be Present ~ Therapy ~ Forgive and Let Go

Your mind is a powerful thing. Your mind will shape your perceptions, decide how you will react (or *not* react), and help you find peace. By working on your incredible mind, you will be able to navigate through your divorce with clarity. You will do this by being positive, present, and by exercising forgiveness and letting go. Therapy can also be helpful to understand how your mind works and how to process the feelings from your divorce. All will help you strengthen your incredible mind.

<u>Stay Positive</u>

Staying positive will help with your divorce and your life. Unless you have a rockin' prenup and a compliant ex, everything about divorce reeks of "negative." Divorce is a shitty time in your life, and it is okay to feel that way. That's why it is even more important to stay positive. Problem-solving in a productive way helps minimize the destruction divorce can create. You can come up with solutions that might otherwise evade you.

Staying positive can be difficult – there are negative things all around you. You may find that some people avoid those who are divorced. You may find that your family members disapprove of your choice to get divorced or blame you for the other person divorcing you. If you have children, they may lash out at you by saying "Why couldn't you two work it out?" "You've ruined everything!" "I HATE YOU!"

While we cover a lot of areas to help you make your divorce a more positive one, some are more challenging than others. What can you do to stay strong and positive RIGHT NOW? The first step is to change how your mind is looking at the divorce. Remember these things:

1. It is not your fault. We do not care who cheated on who. The past is the past. It takes two to get married, and it takes two to get divorced.
2. Do not blame yourself.
3. Envision your new life in a positive way. Look beyond the divorce.
4. Believe in taking the "high road." Prepare your mind for this. Make your words and actions match.

Divorce can be a positive thing. Really? Yes, Really! That is what this book is about. Keep a positive outlook about the divorce and the pieces will fall into place.

Note from Leah...

I have worked hard to stay positive through my divorce. I will admit some days it is really hard to keep moving forward, but I always manage to pull through, and you will too. It is important to realize that today is a new day. Live in this moment. It is not the time to worry about yesterday or what was. It is wasted energy. Focus on the things in life you are thankful for right now. For example your health, children, including fur babies, family, and friends. Practice gratitude. Look for the positive in your life, and remember the mindful breathing section.

Note from Robin...

I spent too much time "in" my divorce after my divorce was finalized. I found a solution in daydreaming about a life where I would no longer have to deal with court dates, custody battles, or the ex. By daydreaming about my desired future, I found it much easier to stay positive.

I imagined my future life in Spain, Argentina, or Canada. Envisioning that future helped keep me positive. I began to understand the difficulties I was going through were temporary. The difficult times would pass. I would get through this.

Activity: We challenge you to think about what is bothering you most at this moment. Now, visualize the outcome you would like to see. Try and feel that moment, visualize your surroundings, facial expressions, etc. Practicing this will help. Do this when you are worried or stressed about an upcoming situation. Visualize the positive outcome you desire.

Be Present!

When is the next court date? What will the ex say next? Is there something I could have done differently in my marriage?

"Should have's," "What if's," and other worries about the past and future will only distract and aggravate you. Replaying events you could have handled differently will undermine your self-confidence. Worrying about scenarios that may happen in the future can cause you to become obsessive, suspicious, and untrusting, causing you to over-react to the most innocent of situations.

Although you should always be thinking ahead, there is a high possibility your mindset will get out of control while you are going through a divorce. With the added stress of divorce, life is busy, and things just became a whole lot busier if you are a single parent or no longer part of a couple.

A friend of ours always says, "It is what it is!" She is a master at being present. During her divorce, she kept calm and let things take their course. She said the way to happiness was to live in the moment and be present for each day. She recognized that the divorce could last years, but she did not want to miss a single day of her children growing up. By being present, she was a better parent and did not experience the same degree of stress and worry some of our other friends did.

Try not to let the hectic aspects of life clog up your daily wellbeing. Take a moment to walk outside and smell the fresh air or hear the birds chirping. Be present in the events happening *right now*. Notice the things around you, the beauty of where you live, the seasons changing or colors of the trees, the ocean. Whatever it may be, take a moment to appreciate the world. It is these small moments that will help you to clear your head and be present in your life. Remember, you are starting a new chapter in life – be present for it. Your incredible mind will appreciate it.

Note from Leah...

Time and again I have to tell myself to be present in the moment. It is all too easy to get tangled in a web of thoughts. *What do I need to do? Why is this happening like this? How am I going to handle this alone?* The list goes on and on. When this happens, I tell myself to STOP. Take a moment to breathe and to remind myself that it will be okay. I handle things in small doses. If you let your thoughts get the best of you, then you can't get anything done. It is like being in a fog. I know this from experience, so I practice daily to control my thoughts to be fully present in the moment.

When you are present, the world seems clearer. The sky is more vibrant, the birds seem louder, and you notice the smell of the ocean or air when you're in the moment. It feels good to notice these things and feel connected to the earth. When my thoughts are too distracted with the past or future, I force myself to take a moment and take in the world around me. Try it. It works.

Note from Robin...

Spinning. That is how I describe not being present. When I'm spinning, I'm thinking too much about what happened months ago. I think too much about what may happen. This spinning into the past and future does nothing but put me off balance. There is nothing I can do to change the past, and there are outcomes beyond my control.

Not being in the present also makes me act paranoid. Is my ex cruising by my house again? Why did he say that? Bringing myself back to center, into the present, keeps me from being stressed. I focus on what is directly in front of me rather than on things I can't change.

Activity: Learn to let it go. Close your eyes. Breathe. Let go of all the thoughts racing through your head. Focus on something peaceful. Do this when you need to be fully present.

Get Therapy

Although it can be expensive, the right therapist can be invaluable. During therapy, you will learn more about your mind and how it works, how you react to situations, and why you interact with your spouse a certain way. By speaking with an experienced professional, you will be able to give your incredible mind extra strength to handle this part of your life.

Getting a therapist is something you should do sooner rather than later. A divorce can be an emotionally traumatic event. Your mind needs an outlet so you can remain balanced and sane during this time. Having a therapist will help you gain the necessary skills to cope with the emotional roller coaster you will be going through. A therapist can offer an objective and reasonable perspective as you are transitioning out of your marriage. Having friends can help, but they are not therapists. Even if you put your friends on rotation to not wear any person out, your friends can only do so much.

Since you are dealing with a divorce, look for a therapist familiar with custody battles and divorces. Experienced therapists who work with clients in divorce can give advice that best serves your interests and the best interests of your children. Your therapist can do much more than help you feel better, and they will also provide valuable advice on how to handle your ex. A good therapist during divorce is someone who will also give you the tools to deal with a difficult ex while supporting you through this emotionally draining journey.

Note from Leah...

Having a therapist can be a good idea while you're married, too. I believe that therapy earlier in my marriage would have made things smoother. It is a good idea to invest in yourself and talk to an expert. Everyone has issues. It is good to have a professional to help you along through life no matter what you are going through.

One of my friends was told to see a therapist by her attorney. This therapist helped give her extremely good advice and helped her recognize that she was going through a high-conflict custody battle. As a result, she was able to gather additional resources to help her through the situation.

Note from Robin...

Having a therapist can help in any difficult situation. I've found my own therapist to be a wonderful guide, advisor, and sympathetic sounding board. With divorce, you may find that your family has alienated you, your ex has accused you of cheating, and your children accuse you of being abusive for having them do homework and going to bed at a decent hour.

You are not alone. This situation has happened to more than one friend of ours. A therapist can show you that your family members may be acting out on old resentments from childhood. An ex who is spreading lies about you may be trying to gather sympathy from others instead of acknowledging his or her own failings in the marriage. Children? What child doesn't try to play one parent against the other to get away with a later bedtime or less homework? A therapist can help guide you through these difficult situations and make your divorce easier on you.

Activity: Go online and research therapists in your area or ask friends. Look for people who have experience with divorce. You don't have to call a therapist right now, but the information will be there if you need it.

<u>Forgive and Let Go</u>

There are some things you will not be able to control. One of those things is your ex. You will not be able to control what they say about you, what they think about you, and how they behave. You will not be able to control the legal process if they become litigious and decide to sue you over things like the children's bedtime or whether or not the children should take ballet or kung fu. In fact, your ex may be acting crazy because the EX has lost control over YOU.

You will need to let go of a lot of things. Divorce is a roller coaster, not a merry-go-round. There will be ups and downs. You will get used to them. Control the things you can. Let the other stuff go. Letting go includes letting go of the snide comments your ex may have made or forgiving your ex for cheating on you.

Are we asking a lot? Yes. But, you can do it.

What happens if you don't? During one of our trips, we encountered a person who could not forgive and let go. This man went on and on about his ex-wife and all the horrible things she did to him. When we asked him how long ago they divorced, he said it was twelve years ago. Twelve years?! That man was a person whose mind was still preoccupied with his ex, even though the relationship was over long ago. He offered to buy us a round of drinks, but we politely declined.

Many of the things that you are stressing about now will not matter much in the future. The ex forgot his mother's birthday, did not remember the children's recital or gave you a smirk while you were walking out of court. You help the kids pick out meaningful gifts for the ex's birthday, but your ex takes them to the Dollar Store to pick out *your* gift and makes them pay for it.

These are little things. Let them go. Even cheating is a little thing because you're no longer with that person and you will never be with them again. Keep an eye on the end game. You're done with that relationship and it is time to move on. Your incredible mind can forgive and let go.

Note from Leah…

Letting go is important to do, and you are probably wondering, "How in the world do I forgive when people can be such asses?!" Yes, my thoughts exactly!

When I was still living in the home while separated, it was probably the worst four months of my life. Fortunately, I had a friend who bought me a book that helped me heal during this time. It was after reading this book that I was able to see things clearly. The book helped me to understand that some things just are not meant to last and to let go of the guilt. Letting go allows you to move on.

Forgiveness and letting go can be hard to do when you're in the thick of a divorce, and everything seems to be crumbling around you. I'm here to say things will get better if you change your intentions and thoughts during this process. Yes, this is hard to do when you are so angry with your former significant other and upset with whatever they are doing to make things hard on you. You have to learn to let it go.

A mentor of mine once told me, "It won't matter in a year from now." It is hard to process, but my mentor was right. Whatever that issue was, it didn't matter later. So learn not to take things personally and let it go. Just remember you are on the way to a much happier life, and let that thought guide you.

Note from Robin...

Someone once told me, "I can't forgive my mom until she says she is sorry." That is counterproductive. Forgiveness is not something you give to someone else. It is not bartered, bargained for, or given with conditions. Forgiveness is something you give *yourself.*

She also said that she could forgive her ex for a lot of things. However, she had a hard time forgiving and letting go because of what her kids went through. I told her that it's not her forgiveness – that belongs to the kids. If they feel wronged, they will give the forgiveness.

And with that, I let it go.

Activity: On a sheet of paper list four things that are bothering you most at this moment. Now, rip it up into many pieces, and let it go.

Your Resilient Spirit

Appreciate the Small Things ~ Music & Dance ~ I am Free

During a divorce, your spirit may seem crushed. There will be many occasions where you will feel like you have been run over by a freight train. You may be exhausted. You may be depressed. Your spirit may feel battered, but your spirit will survive. These are some of the ways to keep your spirit aligned and uplifted.

Appreciate The Small Things

There are a lot of big events going on. You are making life-changing decisions. You could be encountering hostility from your ex. You may have some friends or family that do not understand why you are getting divorced. And life will go on and continue to be busy while your world feels like it's falling apart. With all the changes you are going through, life can appear overwhelming and unstable.

Appreciating the small things will make the big things less daunting. Remember: *small* things. By small, we mean minuscule. Appreciate the sunrise or the sunset. Appreciate the clean air you breath or the clean sheets fresh out of the dryer. Keep appreciating the small things and the big things will seem simpler.

When you take the time to appreciate the small things, you realize how good you have it. You have clean water. You have a roof over your head. These are things that some people don't have. If you have kids, they are good at putting the small things into perspective. Notice the joy a child has when playing in the park? The park is free. Notice the joy they have when they have an ice cream cone with sprinkles? Something so small and simple gives them such joy. How happy we would all be if we all took the time to appreciate the small things.

Take a step back in time and see things from a child's point of view. See how their spirit is free. Try to emulate that. Appreciate those small things: the air, the comfort of your blanket, or a sip of cool water. Enjoy them fully and appreciate them heartily – it is when we appreciate the small things that the big things lose ground and are replaced with the tiny joys that positively impact our life every day.

Note from Leah...

Recently, where I live, the season was changing. San Diego has mild season changes but, still, there were leaves on the ground. My son was soooo excited about how big the leaves were on the ground and the crunching noise they made as he stomped on them. It took this moment for me to appreciate the smaller things in life like my ability to jump on those leaves with him, and even more fun, to jump in the rain puddles in the street with him.

I can't express the excitement my two young boys feel when it rains, and there are rain puddles around to jump in. If you have young children, you can probably relate. Their excitement is contagious. It will not be long before they are grown, so it is important to enjoy these little moments in time and to be mindful and appreciate the small things.

Note from Robin...

I had a difficult time appreciating the small things during part of my divorce. *Everything* seemed big, monstrous, and scary. Even the smallest things that went wrong would feel like failures on my part. I felt like I was breaking.

Taking a step back, I started to look at small things I *could* appreciate. I had to start with the ridiculous: I appreciated that toilet paper was still on the roll in the bathroom. Why? Because I was the only one using that bathroom now. Why? Because I left that guy, who used so much toilet paper. Why? Because I wanted something better in my life. All of a sudden, the small appreciation of toilet paper turned into a big appreciation of the turning point of my life, and the realization that I was a worthy person who deserved better.

Activity: Create a list of the ten things that pop into your mind that you are truly appreciative of right now. Wow, look how fortunate you are! Be grateful.

<u>Music & Dance</u>

When was the last time you danced? How about the last time you listened to music? Have you been spending the past several years watching your children's dance classes and playing toddler music in the car? It's time to surround yourself with music and dance in a way that reflects YOU and your spirit.

Music can be what you play or what you listen to. If you play an instrument, it's time to get back into it. Just try ten minutes. Play the songs from your childhood. It will take you back to a time when your life was simpler. Or, try a new piece that you have wanted to play for a while. While playing, your mind will untangle the mess of thoughts that have accumulated during your divorce. You will feel calmer and emotionally balanced after just a few minutes on your instrument.

One of our friends took up an instrument after his divorce. He decided to play piano because he had always wanted to as a child. With his wife gone, he had a lot of time on his hands. He took lessons for several years and got very good. He felt that music saved his life by giving him an outlet to get through his divorce.

For the music you listen to, let your tunes reflect who YOU are. Get rid of the songs that remind you of your marriage. Heaven forbid if you actually have kept songs to play for the ex. Get rid of those too. Surround yourself with music that will lift you up. Remember, this is an activity to uplift your spirit – what you hear will make its way inside of you so feed yourself the good stuff.

Dancing is fun and, if you grab your friends to go out dancing with you, it's even more so. You will be able to multi-task: exercise *and* socialize. Dancing is therapeutic, good for your soul and body. It releases the tension and stress, and it's a fast calorie burn. It may take a little effort to go out dancing if you haven't been for a while. If you are not the clubbing type, think about trying some different types of dancing. There are groups for line dancing, ballroom, and tap. You can do traditional dancing from all sorts of cultures. Many of these dancing groups don't require partners. Now, you have the advantage of meeting new people and getting exercise.

Note from Leah...

I can't emphasize enough how important and uplifting music can be. I love music! I have it on all day, and it is probably why I want to dance all the time. It really can help you in all sorts of ways. Once I moved into my new place, I realized I could listen to all the music that *I liked all day long*. I have a new found love for the genres of music that my ex didn't care for. They are on constant rotation now. It uplifts my mood almost instantly and even helps me to feel sexy when needed.

It is scientifically backed that music is therapeutic so find your favorite online channels and have them on constant rotation. I grab my girlfriends any chance I get to go out dancing. It's a way to let go of all the worries for an hour or two and truly enjoy the moment.

Dance it out!

Note from Robin...

Once upon a time, my ex bought me an iPod. Then, he downloaded every Elvis song in existence as a "favor." I don't listen to Elvis, never have. Do you see why we divorced?

I do have a secret love of country music that was not shared in one of my relationships. It was something I played a lot of. It was a liberating experience not having to cater to my partner's musical whims. Once I got country out of my system, I started branching out and collecting music lists for parts of my day: Bach for the morning, rock and blues before going out with my girlfriends. I even put together a playlist for a girl's weekend, filled with empowering music by strong female musicians.

As for dance, I had a great time going line dancing one night. I jumped right in and tried to follow the group as well as I could. The group absolutely kicked my butt since they were all much more experienced dancers than I was. They were also all over the age of 65. Even so, I had a great time, was happy, and out of breath after only one song.

Activity: Make your personal playlist to uplift your mood and dance to it!

I Am Free

You have the freedom to be you. Do you know who "you" really are? Have you even thought about it lately? It is all too easy to get caught up in the various roles one plays in marriage, to the point that you forget who you really are. Once you are free, you can rediscover yourself.

The feeling of being free comes at you in waves. It is likely that you have been raked over the coals in some way or another during the divorce. However, there are small moments that you will stop and think, "I AM FREE." In these moments you will have some clarity about the tough decisions you've made and the future decisions you're contemplating.

Being free can feel strange. You may feel weightless, not grounded. That strange feeling you're having is freedom. With freedom comes the ability to move in any direction *you* choose such as a new location, towards a new job, or a new relationship.

You're going to have this feeling of weightlessness for a while until you learn to fly on your own. You will make mistakes. Learn your lessons and move on. It is absolutely ok to mess up. If you are not making some mistake at least once a month, then you are not really growing as a person. You will need to push the boundaries of what you are capable of. Growth is what freedom gives you.

It's now time to lift your spirit and find the real you. It may be that you haven't seen the real you since you were a teenager, and that's okay. You are re-inventing a new better version of yourself. You are much wiser and more experienced today. It's time to enjoy your freedom.

Note from Leah...

I continually reflect on various moments in the past year, and there have been several moments where I thought, "I AM FREE." I am free to travel. I am free to go on dates. I am free to jump in the car and see a friend without asking anyone.

After the separation, when I first moved into my new home, the move-out day was horrible. Once the movers unloaded the truck and left, it was time to start putting together my new home. One of the first things I hung up was a chalkboard over my desk. I purchased it intending to put inspiring quotes on it. I also purchased this fancy coffee shop chalk to write with, so I could make it look creative. That afternoon I hung up my fancy chalkboard and wrote: "I am free." It felt good to make such a statement and have it posted on the wall.

As time went on, I decided that I wanted to change it to a new inspiring quote. I tried to erase it, and it would not erase. I tried using all kinds of techniques to erase it, but nothing worked. I even tried lemon oil, and it works on everything, but it only dimmed it. Finally, I gave up and realized I need that reminder on my wall. I still look at it daily and am thankful for the reminder that I Am Free to live my life how I choose.

Note from Robin...

I had terrible back problems for almost a year before asking for the divorce. I was in a brace, went to the doctor, went to the chiropractor, tried massages, everything. The day I asked for the divorce, my back problems disappeared. I didn't realize the tension I had been holding in my body as a result of being unhappy.

I will never forget the relief I felt once I separated from my ex. Once he left, I felt immediately uplifted, my back was fine, and I was free.

Activity: Look in the mirror, each day, for 30 days and say, "I am FREE."

Your Outer Influences

Energy Vampires ~ The Right People ~ The Right Places ~ Support Groups

What and whom you surround yourself with have a tremendous effect on the inner you. These are your outer influences. Some of the most successful people in the world surround themselves with the best people: the best financial advisors, legal help, and business mentors. You are a work in progress; surround yourself with the right influences to create your work of art – YOU.

Beware of Energy Vampires

We start with a very important type of person you should *not* surround yourself with – an energy vampire. An energy vampire is someone that sucks the life out of you. They use up all your time and drain your energy. They can even use up all of your money. They leave you empty after taking the best of you. Then, they wait. They wait for you to recharge yourself and then they do it again. In the end, you have to remove yourself from their drama and, ultimately, no matter how much you try to help that person, it will not work.

It is absolutely important to divorce an energy vampire. This type of person needs to look within and help themselves. If you continue to let them feed off your energy, they will take all they can.

One of our friends had an ex who was an energy vampire. The ex would create a lot of conflicts, even after separation. The tiniest little transgression on her part, even if it was not responding to an email right away, created huge issues with her ex. At first, she kept jumping whenever he called, emailed, or texted about the most mundane things.

We sat down with her and showed her how these constant interruptions during her day were negatively influencing her life. We explained that if it was not an urgent matter, she could respond later. If she handled all the issues at one sitting, she could have peace of mind for the rest of the day. At first, her ex was extremely mad that she was not feeding into his demands immediately when he contacted her. After two months of "starving" her energy vampire, he got used to the new schedule, and the constant interruptions stopped.

During divorce, if the vampire is your ex, they are not done with you. The vampire has tasted your blood, and it has become a regular part of their daily diet. They will want more, especially since you have cut off their main supply. They will continue to try to draw blood by striking out at you, making you bleed. Then they suck up the blood you spill in the form of anger, frustration, and bitterness.

Starve them. Do not give them any of those negative emotions that feed their souls. Keep your interactions civil and brief.

Note from Leah...

The energy vampire can be lurking, and you are not even aware of it. It could be a good friend or even a family member. Time and again, I have been able to sniff these people out pretty well. Still, once in a while, I get blindsided by one. It is important to acknowledge their bad energy and learn to distance yourself from it. There are various ways to go about doing this including limiting contact, setting boundaries, and in some instances cutting them out of your life entirely. I know that may seem harsh, but they will suck you dry if you do not set such boundaries.

I had a friend that introduced this concept to me. My friend had to "divorce" a friend due to her negative energy. I had never heard this term utilized this way before. I thought it was an interesting concept, and such an appropriate term to divorce a friend. Now I know this may be hard to do if the person you are divorcing is a person close to you, but you can still limit contact. It is okay to distance yourself from people that are negative or looking to bring you down.

Note from Robin...

I've had to resist the urge to feed into others need for pity. I have found myself in situations where someone plays the victim, in spite of knowing what the consequences of their actions are. My former self would have indulged someone like that in feeling sorry for himself. Now, I don't. I don't apologize, neither do I accuse.

One thing you have to remember when you cut off someone's supply, is that you will experience his or her rage. Think of it like a drug addict, and you are the supplier. They have money to pay, good money, and *you won't give it to them.*

Do not give in to them. Not giving in will be challenging and you will experience all sorts of accusations, criticism, and possible name-calling. But if you give in, the cycle starts all over again. The best you can do is to stop being their emotional drug dealer. They will never stop. They need their fix. Close up shop and let them take their business elsewhere.

Activity: Make a list of the energy vampires in your life. Put them on a diet.

<u>Surround Yourself with the Right People</u>

Now we can move on to the types of people you *should* surround yourself with. Have people around who are positive. These are people who lift your spirits instead of bringing you down. Nothing likes misery more than miserable people. Keep those people out of your life. The right people are the ones that are going to put things in perspective for you when you are too much in the thick of things to see clearly. These are the people that will make you laugh when you are about to cry. They will help you find joy and fun in your life. They will call you out on your bullshit or let you know that you are being taken advantage of when you can not see it yourself. They will also help you see the humor in situations.

The saying *"Your tribe is your vibe"* is a powerful statement. Think about what that means to you: Who are the top people in your life? Why? What kind of people are they? Are they positive thinkers? Negative? Do they complain a lot or always make you laugh in their presence? Surround yourself with positive, like-minded people. The right people will give you a lift. The wrong people will bring you down.

A man we were speaking with was just separating from his wife. He talked about how his friend was also getting a divorce at the same time. His friend's divorce was pretty nasty. Talking to his friend seemed to make his divorce even worse. He took his friend's negative energy and transferred it to his divorce. He eventually cut down his contact with his negative friend and found that his divorce went much more smoothly. He then found a group of other people who were having a more positive divorce experience. He chose to surround himself with more positive influences, which helped him have a better divorce experience.

This example shows that the right people will also include people who have experienced divorce recently. They will be a great resource for attorneys, accountants, and babysitters. They will be able to give you an idea of the path you are walking, warn you of pitfalls, and comfort you when you fall. They have lived it, survived, and they are there for you now. The positive people you surround yourself with will support you and give you strength.

Note from Leah...

There are many stages you go through when getting divorced, and having a good support system is crucial. You have the initial breakup, the separation, the serving of papers, the move-out date, and all that comes after you're separated. After the move-out, the new life, and new changes can take a toll on you in many different ways. It is important to have positive people surrounding you, to keep you grounded and to uplift you when needed.

For example, one of my friend's was having a meltdown with the stress of work, finances, the divorce being stagnant, and her ex-husband not being nice. She had a moment of weakness to the point that she wasn't even sure what to tackle first. She left a message for a friend who instantly called back and talked her through that moment.

Different friends will step up at different points as needed during this time. You will realize you have the power to change all of these situations, and likely in a good position to do it once acknowledging it. So, sometimes it takes a person from the outside who cares about you to help you see clearly in moments when you don't know where to move next. It is essential to surround yourself with these uplifting, positive people who will not let you down during hard times.

Note from Robin...

I discovered there were people in my life who were negative influences during my divorce. They dragged me down and left me tired. They kept me in a cycle of negativity. I slowly replaced those people with positive support. Replacing these people was difficult but necessary. I couldn't function with negative people in my life.

Now, I surround myself with more positive people. I have some friends that are wonderful in small doses and great to hang out with every once and a while. There are friends that I rely on every day, or every week to get me through this time in my life. The more positive and supportive the friend is, the more frequently I want to be around them. Being surrounded by positive people has made the divorce process easier.

Activity: Create a list of the five people closest to you. What type of energy do they display? (i.e. negative, complaining, positive, happy) Now, write a list of the five people in your life that have positive energy. It may be that you have never thought about the type of vibe your tribe is putting off. Knowing is half the battle!

Be in the Right Place

Being in the right place is the best way to be open to positive outer influences. It is difficult to feel positive when you are physically in the wrong place. For example, do not try to have a conversation with your ex when you are in line at the DMV. If you are in a house that has conflict or that isn't safe, remove yourself from that place. Where you are will do a lot to influence your actions and reactions.

You do not need negative places. Divorce has enough negativity. If it takes moving out of an area of conflict, do it. Negative surroundings have a way of seeping into your spirit and wearing you down. You need to be in a safe, positive place to keep your spirit up and to keep yourself strong. Be in the right place, not the negative place.

Connecting with nature is a way to feel more positive by being in the right place. It will help you get in touch with yourself and help remove negativity. Go for a hike, a beach walk, or even a walk around a park. Make an effort to get outside and go for a walk. During this walk, breathe in the fresh air.

Being in the right place also means being in a place where the people are supportive and kind. The right place can be a quiet place, your home, or any other safe place where you can surround yourself with positive people and energy. A place where you can meditate, relax, and think will give you time to recharge and reflect.

Note from Leah...

Be in the right place can mean different things. It can mean something like removing yourself from one room into another or heading outside. It can be bigger than that. It can mean moving out of the house you were in with your ex.

For a friend of mine, there was conflict surrounding who would move out of the house. She took the higher road and found herself a smaller place nearby. The feeling of being out of the previous home filled with such toxic energy was the most freeing thing she could have done. She created a new space that was all her own. She created her sanctuary. It was the best decision she could have made.

Note from Robin...

I now take the time to surround myself with positive people and places that will help me feel better about myself.

Sometimes I need to surround myself with chatty friends, other times with blissful solitude. I'm continually amazed how QUIET things are when I am in a place where I can think. It seems like the whole world slows down and I can sense the quiet passage of time. When I am in this space, I have clarity and peace.

Activity: Make a list of safe places. They should be places that leave you feeling calm, happy, content and peaceful.

<u>Find a Support Group</u>

A support group can be one of your most powerful outer influences. A support group will affect the way you handle your divorce, deal with your ex, and move towards a more peaceful life. You will need the right type of support to help you build up your life after the tearing down of your marriage. You need someone to listen, not judge. You need someone to give advice, not admonish.

You will gain an incredible amount of insight when listening to others who have walked the path you are on, right now. No matter how much your friends and family listen to you, a support group will offer a different kind of support: the support of someone outside your usual social circle. They will be able to provide advice or suggestions that your friends and family might not be able or willing to give.

There are support groups for all sorts of situations. Some are organized through religious organizations or community resources. Others are formed through online connections. There are support groups for people who are recently divorced, or for people who are married and trying to make it work. There are support groups for people who are single, or single with kids. If you have a disease or disorder, there's a support group for you. If you just want to hang out, you can find a group for that too.

Support groups are the best type of free therapy out there. Sometimes it can be better than therapy because you will connect with individuals who are in the same situation you are in. Best of all, you will find that your position is not unique. A support group will lessen the anxiety and stress divorce may cause you. After a while, each story you hear will sound eerily like your own. Knowing you are not alone can be comforting.

Note from Leah...

I am fortunate to have great friends in my life, and I believe every person comes into your life for a reason. I have not been to an organized support group. However, I have many girlfriends who have been my personal support group. It may not be an organized group that you attend, but you will find that you can call on friends who have had similar experiences for advice. You may find that you randomly meet a group of people who have gone through similar situations that share some insights. Time and again I have met people in the most random of ways who are going through similar situations, so be open minded to new sources of support.

It is crazy how you can instantly feel a connection with someone based on the experiences you have shared. You can run into someone in line at the bathroom or chat with someone online and find you have shared experiences. There is always something new to learn from new people. Stay open minded. Things happen for a reason.

Note from Robin…

I have been a part of a support group for many years. I consider some of the members of my support group some of my dearest friends. People I have met there know more about my marriage than my friends and family ever will. They know my strengths and have heard of my fears and sorrows. They have seen each step I have made towards being a better person. It has been a life changing experience to be a part of a group of people with similar experiences, even though we are of all different ages and backgrounds.

Activity: Research a support group in your area. It can be divorce related or related to some other issue that you've had in your life. Try at least one meeting.

Chapter Two

FAMILY MATTERS

A divorce does not only involve two people. There are side players involved such as children, in-laws, and mutual friends. Everyone you know will feel the effects of your divorce. If your divorce is friendly, this will be a smooth process. There may be some uncomfortable situations around the holidays, but if everyone can move on from the relationship, there should be minimal conflict.

If you are unfortunate enough to have what is known as a high-conflict divorce, family matters will feel more like a war zone. In-laws will freeze you out, friends will choose sides, and parents fighting will hurt the children. Financial devastation is likely from high legal fees, and it will take years to recover emotionally. We offer some ways to minimize and hopefully avoid conflict altogether.

On this journey through divorce, we've met many people with similar stories. One consistent theme is finding that extended families don't know how to react when someone they know gets divorced. You may find yourself in a similar situation. It may even be your own family that takes sides with your ex. It can happen, so you need to be aware of the possibility.

This chapter will start with the right attitude to have when dealing with family matters, from getting through the hard stuff to remaining kind to the family even when they make you mad. We will share stories about children and their ability to get through the divorce. We will also discuss the dreaded ex, the in-laws, and other family members. You will find many other people who have had similar experiences as your own.

Attitude is Everything

The Hard Stuff ~ Kindness Matters ~ Time Outs

You have heard it again and again: Attitude is everything. With family matters, your attitude will affect how many of those relationships play out. You are in a place in your life when the last thing you want is a pep talk. Don't worry. This is not that talk. We are offering practical ways to handle stressful situations and de-escalate hostility. It starts with how to act and react. The rest will fall into place naturally.

<u>Get Through the Hard Stuff</u>

Divorce is one of the most painful experiences you will have. Understanding that it's difficult is the first step towards having the right attitude. Don't wallow in self-pity. You are not the first person who has been divorced, and you will not be the last. The sooner you move into acceptance, the sooner you will be able to have the proper attitude to deal with those closest to you. Remember, divorce is an emotionally driven event, and your family will be drawn into it. The bottom line is that you will never get to happiness until you get through the hard stuff.

So what is the hard stuff? The hard stuff is experiencing all the emotions that need to be processed. We are emotionally based beings. We hurt. We feel. We heal. When we are hurt, we need to let those feelings happen, or else we will never heal. You may feel anger, shame, depression, anxiety, and many other emotions before you are truly finished with the divorce. Some people take years to get through it, and some never get through it at all. Your challenge is to get through it as quickly as possible so you can move on with your life.

One of our friends went through a particularly troubling custody dispute with her ex. The process lasted nearly three years and cost her hundreds of thousands of dollars. When we asked her how she got through it, she said, "I knew that the difficult times were temporary. I kept saying to myself that it was just a phase. I kept my eye on the future and just wanted what was best for my kids." She knew that her kids would appreciate her efforts in the future. As it turns out, the kids no longer talk to their dad because of the conflict he put them through during the divorce.

It will get better once you get through the hard stuff. Many people will say "the grass is not greener on the other side" with regards to divorce. This is an untrue statement. Everyone has their view of things, and they do not know what struggles you are going through in your marriage. Do not be ashamed that you could not make it work. The universe has a plan for you, and you are meant to move on to bigger and better things.

Cry, stomp, rage, scream. Do these things and *then be done with it.* It is only when you process those emotions that you can move on with the right attitude. What is that attitude? YOU CAN GET THROUGH THIS.

Note from Leah...

In college, I worked in various restaurants. It is common in the restaurant world to go into the walk-in refrigerator and scream at the top of your lungs when you are having a bad night. I did this, and it helped! It also helped that it was a well-enclosed freezer so no one could hear. Find your version of the walk-in freezer and let it out, whether it be screaming, crying or just tearing something up. To truly let go, you need to allow yourself to feel the hurt.

The hurt does not need to be forever. Those feelings are part of the healing pattern. But by holding on to anger or a grudge all you are doing is keeping yourself stuck in the past. YOU have to forgive, understand the marriage has ended, and feel the hurt so you can truly let go and move on.

Note from Robin...

Even though I was the one who asked for the divorce, I still had to mourn for the marriage. Mourning took some time. During that process, I had to let myself feel anger and disappointment. I began to realize that I had held a lot of these feelings down to try to make my marriage work. These feelings were not always directed towards my ex, some of them were directed towards myself. Why didn't I leave earlier?

After I was free from the marriage, I was also free to feel suppressed emotions. My anger eventually turned to pity and then to ambivalence towards the people who hurt me. I began to plan my future. My attitude shifted towards me. What I wanted in my life took priority. It was only when I got through the hard stuff that I was able to adjust my attitude and put more focus on my family and myself.

Activity: Make a list of all the things from the past you are holding on to... anger, resentment, or guilt? List them, read them out loud, and then rip up the page and let it go. Free yourself.

<u>Kindness Matters</u>

Kindness matters when dealing with your family in the divorce. As we mentioned before, divorce is an emotionally charged event. You will simultaneously be dealing with your own emotions and those your family is going through. Being kind will remind everyone that a peaceful resolution is the best and the least damaging for all.

Even so, divorce can be nasty for most people. As much as you want your ex to get what your ex deserves in the end, it does not prove anything. In fact, putting so much effort into proving someone wrong can escalate the conflict. If kids are involved, it is even more important to take the high road. Kindness means not talking poorly about your ex in front of your kids. Remind them that you are still a team because otherwise, the kids could experience anxiety and stress. Be mindful that this process affects them just as much you but in a way that they will have difficulty understanding.

Having an attitude of kindness towards any adversary is an exercise in benevolence. It is also the most efficient and humane way to close a relationship. Kindness requires consistently monitoring your words. You know your ex, and you know the words that can set them off. As tempting as it is, keep your attitude in kindness mode. Otherwise, you will find yourself on the defensive when the attacks come from the other direction.

Our friend who went through the long custody battle also explained how kindness mattered in her custody dispute with her ex. "I didn't like him," she said. "In fact, I hated him. But I could be *friendly* with him, even though I wasn't friends with him." She was so kind that her ex's attorney had a difficult time painting her as the angry, vindictive ex-wife that her ex claimed she was. In the end, it worked in her favor regarding custody of the children.

If your family or in-laws are not supportive of you, kindness will seem nearly impossible. You may want to lash out at them for choosing sides. In that case, concentrate on kind *actions*. Continue to participate in family events and send birthday cards and small gifts to family members. After a time, they may come around. If not, you have done your part. The divorce is easier for everyone when you remember that kindness matters. Most importantly, kindness will make the divorce easier on you.

Note from Leah...

Having children involved makes everything in divorce more complicated. It is even more challenging with young children. It is important to ensure they know you are still a family. My son once asked me, *"Mom, why did you and dad get a divorce?"* I answered, *"Daddy and I still love you more than anything, but we get along better living in different homes"* followed by, *"We will always be a family and a team."* This was the first time after the separation that my 8-year-old son asked me this question. I had to choose my words wisely and ultimately wanted my child to know that we were still kind towards one another.

This is also your goal for the children during this process. First and foremost, make sure they know they are loved unconditionally. It is easy to get caught up in the divorce so for the kids' sake, and for you, take the higher road <u>always</u>. Be kind.

Note from Robin...

Sometimes being kind means keeping communications brief. I find that keeping things short and factual is the best way to communicate with an ex. This is especially effective when someone is sending harsh and accusatory emails. If your ex is kind, it is easier to respond with kindness. If your ex is hostile, it is best to answer briefly and firmly. There is less room for error and misinterpretation of your words when you use fewer of them.

Activity: Create a "Kindness Journal." Write down ways you can show kindness to others.

<u>Time Outs</u>

Remember "time outs" when you were a kid? They typically happened when you were having a rough day and then acted out in some way. Your parent would put you in a corner or in a chair to calm down. The benefit was that you would have time to gather your thoughts and think about what just happened. We recommend that you take "time outs" when you need time to think. This parenting trick from your childhood can help you through your divorce, especially when dealing with difficult family members.

By way of example, the ex just said something nasty, your mother asks why you couldn't have stayed married, and your best friend has gone AWOL. This is a time when you need to think about your relationships with them and remain calm. Your automatic reactions are not always the best ones when you are going through a divorce. Emotions are heightened, and you are sensitive to criticism. Take a "time out" and gather your thoughts before you react to an emotional situation.

If you have kids, you know that being a single parent is hard. You have not had time to grow into the role of parenting on your own. You will adjust and get into a new rhythm. Although you may have given your fair share of Time Outs to your children, it is important that you take time for yourself to recharge, think and remain calm. This is where a personal Time Out is great. Just tell your kids, "I'm going to Time Out!" If you are going to be a good parent, you need to be in a good place mentally.

Note from Leah...

It is absolutely okay to take a time out for yourself. This may include booking a day at the spa or shopping. I love shopping both alone and with friends. I found over the years shopping was therapeutic for me. I do not always have the funds to buy things, but even the browsing has its benefits. It also helps when having a bad day or confronting the reality of life as a single parent.

It is tough being a single parent and time outs will help. It is essential to allow yourself a break. It will help you remain calm and collected during tough moments. Being the mother of two very active young boys has its challenges. I often tell my kids when I get to this point that 'mommy needs a time out' and this will typically lighten the mood.

When I do say this to my kids, the roles seem to change. All of the sudden, they are trying to help improve *my* mood. Maybe the act of saying it out loud is all that is needed at the moment. "Mommy's on a time-out!" If that doesn't work, there is always wine!

Note from Robin...

Opening emails from certain people can be a source of anxiety for me. So, I have a 24-hour rule when dealing with those emails. This is my "time out." My fingers itch to draft a cutting email back. Instead, I wait. The rule is that I need to sleep on it. While I am waiting, I come up with all sorts of sarcastic things to say and points to make to show that I think that person is an asshole. As I think about it, the proposed email gets shorter and shorter until it is nothing but an acknowledgment of the information given or a brief, factual answer to a question. I realize that some people try to engage me in an argument and the best way to handle it is to disengage.

Activity: Schedule an activity just for you. Take a nap, bath, walk on the beach or get your toes done. It is time for a 'Just me' timeout.

Children

Will They Survive? ~ Parenting Class ~ Resources

When children are involved, it puts the divorce on a whole new level. Emotions run high when dealing with the little ones and conflict escalates when one parent attempts to use the children to get back at the other. Don't ever do that.

Your children never asked for the divorce. As a parent, you will need to help them through it by using all resources available. Helping includes therapy, parenting classes, online help, and support from your community.

Will They Survive?

Ideally, parents should be able to work out their differences and remain married. Realistically, some differences are too difficult to reconcile. The children will pick up on your unhappiness, even if you stay in the marriage. Staying in a bad situation sets a bad example of what relationships should be like.

The biggest fear for parents who are thinking about divorce is how their children will handle it. First off, your kids will survive – they are resilient. But a lot depends on you. How the children view your interactions with the other parent will have long-lasting consequences on their lives and future relationships, so your attitude when dealing with your ex needs to be spectacular.

There was a friendly divorce we heard of once. A couple with children got divorced. The husband bought a house directly behind the wife's, so they had a shared fence. They created a gate on the shared fence so the kids could run freely between homes, as they chose. Maybe it's an urban legend. But, it would be wonderful if every divorce could work out like that.

How well the kids survive the divorce depends on YOU. You cannot control what the other parent does. You can only control how you behave. Controlling your behavior may mean letting things slide with the ex from time to time for the sake of the kids. It will also mean compromising. A compromise usually means that neither party is happy and that is how you know it's fair. Be prepared to give a little with regards to your ex. For example, let your ex keep the kids an extra hour if they want instead of insisting that drop off is right on time. Or, encourage your child to call the other parent during your time, just to chat.

The "friendly" divorce is the exception rather than the rule. More often than not, parents argue and cannot come to terms after separating. Whatever happens, the kid's welfare comes first. Before taking any action, especially in front of your children, ask yourself, "Is this what is best for *them*?" In doing so, you can help your kids survive the divorce.

Note from Leah...

Your children will be okay. It is important to show them that you are still a team even when it does not feel like it. I am fortunate in this regard because my ex and I were always on the same page when it came to the children, both in the marriage and after. I am grateful this has continued to be the case.

Do your best to set your emotions aside. Do what is best for your children. Just remember that one day they will be older and have a better understanding of the situation. Think of it this way -- you are setting a good example for them now and for years to come.

Note from Robin...

Shielding kids from conflict is necessary. Whatever differences you have with your ex should not be a part of the conversation you have with your children. Children should not be used as messengers between parents, or as spies in the other parents' home. They have enough to deal with without having to deal with two parents who can't get along.

Even if you hate your ex, never let the children know. They see themselves as half of each parent. Each time you criticize the other parent, the child may take it personally. Be kind, or at the very least, courteous when interacting with your ex in front of the children.

Activity: Schedule a fun activity with your kids. It can be the beach, park, etc. Have a fun day and leave all your anxieties and stressors at home.

Take a Parenting Class

Even though you are a great parent, you can gain a lot from attending a parenting class. They should really be labeled, "How to handle your asshole ex." Aside from teaching about parenting, these classes are geared towards conflicts parents have with each other. You will gain insight as to how other parents handle their situations and acquire tools for de-escalating situations you're in with your ex. There is always more to learn, and a parenting class will give you extra information on how to handle the part of your divorce that deals with children.

We knew a woman who took such a class. She was a wonderful parent, and we were wondering why she would need this class. After the class, she shared all the information she learned, and a lot of it had to do with her ex! She came to understand that her ex was drawing the children into their arguments in subtle ways. The class gave her the tools to deflect this behavior and redirect the conversations in such a way that the children would not become involved.

There are times when you want to do something to show what a loser your ex is. For example, the ex didn't call your child on their birthday, or, your ex did not come to their Citizen of the Month ceremony at school. However, these are not opportunities to bash your ex in front of your kid. It is never good for the kid to hear their parent being bashed. It's like you are bashing half of them. Parenting classes will teach you to ask yourself "is this in the best interests of the children?"

You will learn not to excuse the other parents' behavior if their behavior happens to disappoint the kids. Remember, you are not there to mediate the relationship between your children and their parent. If the other parent messes up, do not make excuses. For example, "I am sure daddy was just busy with something at work," or "Maybe her car broke down and that's why she couldn't come." If your ex was a disappointment to you, your ex will be a disappointment to your child. Your child will need to learn to cope with it.

Parenting classes offer practical solutions for problems. For example, there may be times when you do not want to send your kid to the ex's house with a jacket because the jackets keep disappearing and you know you are never going to get them back. If it is cold, give your kid a jacket. Just remind the ex to bring it back. Do not put it on your child to remember.

Parenting classes are offered in most cities with a variety of class times and locations available. It is worth it to go and invest this time in your children. You will gain a lot of insight by watching other parents who attend the class with you. Some parents will be great examples of how to behave; others will show you how bad it can get. Take the lead from the best and use the others as examples of how *not* to behave.

Note from Leah...

Fortunately my ex and I are good at communication about appointments or school activities for the kids. However, there are going to be times when things get missed, and one parent is going to be upset or annoyed. For example, I had a doctor appointment scheduled months in advance for my son. However, it was not until the day before that it popped up on my calendar. I informed my ex about the appointment when I received the notification. I thought I told him about it months ago. It was a true miscommunication, and this happens. These situations will happen to you. During times like this, you just learn to deal. Parenting classes will help facilitate that.

Note from Robin...

Some courts may ask that the parents attend a parenting class. I decided to pre-empt the request by taking the class on my own. We spent maybe 20% of the time on the kids and the rest of the time on the ex. We did role-playing and spoke about the difficulties we were having in the divorce. It showed me that the source of the conflict is the parents, not the kids. The parenting class helped in a situation that came up nearly a year later.

One of the parents in my parenting class talked about how the class had helped her. She said that the class showed her how to ask the right questions. One day, her ex was expecting her to take her daughter to a birthday party for a friend. Her daughter had made the friend through the dad. While they were searching for parking, her daughter complained that she was feeling sick. She wanted to go home instead of going to the party.

The mom felt her ex would be mad about not taking the daughter to the party, but she had to ask herself the right question, "What is best for my daughter?" Should she drag her to a birthday party when she is ill so her ex wouldn't be mad? No way. She did what was best for her daughter, took her home and let her take a nap.

This parent had to deal with the ex later. She didn't regret the decision one bit. The parenting class helped. In the end, asking the right question helped her make the right decision.

Activity: Take a look at parenting classes in your community. If there's a free one, check it out.

Resources

Resources are available to help your children through divorce. One of the most valuable resources is your child's school. School counselors are available to talk to your kids. They are available during school hours to speak with the children and help them through the divorce. Teachers work with your kids every day and are very empathetic about what their students are going through. The faculty at your child's school is also a great resource for referrals in the community in case you need extra help.

If your child is especially troubled by the divorce, consider getting them a therapist. Therapy may seem a little heavy-handed, but a therapist can help your child transition through the first few years of the divorce when things are unstable. Your child's school will have a list of recommended therapists. These professionals are familiar with children in this situation and can be an objective third party your child can rely on. If your divorce becomes high-conflict, the therapist will be able to offer the court valuable insight into how your child actually feels.

Other programs are offered by profit and non-profit organizations. These programs provide online materials, workshops, and can recommend books and articles for parents and children going through a divorce. A quick online search will guide you to the abundance of programs offered by well-known and reliable children's organizations.

Note from Leah...

There are so many resources available to help children. The first step is to do some research. When my husband and I initially separated, I found a book online written for children and the scenario was exactly our situation. The mother was moving out to a new home, and the father was staying in the family home with two young boys. Even the characters had similar hair colors and looks. It explained how the children would be getting a new room at Mom's new home and they would visit both houses.

The overall story was that the parent loved the kids, and it was in no way their fault the parents were getting a divorce. It was a cute story about the children believing their parents were divorcing due to spilled chocolate while they were misbehaving. The boys enjoyed me reading it to them. I feel it helped during their transition. They would talk randomly about how silly it was that the boy thought the divorce happened from spilled chocolate.

I am grateful for finding this book. It was a happy accident. I continued to read the book to the kids during the transition, and it helped. It is important to be aware of how things are affecting your children during this time. Sometimes just a book can help if you are not able to afford a therapist.

Note from Robin...

When my divorce got difficult, both of my children began seeing therapists. Therapy gave them a safe place to voice their concerns with someone who wasn't going to take mom or dad's side. The therapist is there for my kids, not for me.

Even if my kids aren't going through problems with the divorce, they're able to talk to the therapist about problems with friends at school. Although I may give my kids advice about situations, they tend to listen more when their therapist gives the same advice.

Activity: Buy a children's book on divorce.

Extended Family

In-Laws ~ The Ex & The Feet ~ Siblings and Parents ~ The Ex's Future Ex

Family life is about to get more complicated. When you divorce, family members may take sides. Do not think that because you are related to someone that they will automatically hate your ex. Some people who divorce and keep the in-law's as close friends. Others lose their own family members to the ex. If you have children, then your ex is a part of your family for the rest of their lives.

<u>Talk to the in-laws</u>

Keeping the communication lines open with the in-laws is always a good idea, especially if you still have children. Communication will also help put aside any bad rumors the ex may have spread about you. Keep the conversation flowing with the in-laws, even if it's one-sided. Send your in-laws pictures and videos of their grandkids on a regular basis and have the kids call them every once and a while. The in-laws will be grateful that you continue to include them in the family.

We know a woman who consistently did this with her in-laws. She would text pictures of the kids and share the things they were doing. She would make sure the kids called on their birthdays and holidays. After about a year, the in-laws had thawed out. It turned out that her ex was telling his parents that she was making the kids suffer and never did anything fun with them. The in-laws realized that their son's words weren't matching the pictures and phone calls they were getting from their former daughter-in-law.

Finally, the in-laws came over to her side and gave their son a good talking to.

That example shows how your actions can defeat the misconceptions your in-laws may have about you. They will always be a part of your extended family and can be a great advocate for both you and the kids.

Note from Leah...

Family is vital to me, and it was crucial for my children to have a good relationship with our extended family. I also wanted my boys to be close with their grandparents on their father's side so, when the time was right, and things cooled down a bit, I was happy to reignite that relationship with my former in-laws. They will always be family to me even though I am divorced from their son. Just because you are divorcing does not mean you have to divorce the entire family.

Note from Robin...

One of my friends kept the children in touch with their grandparents and continued this practice after divorce. Even though she knew her ex was telling his mother things about her that were untrue, she never talked badly about him and always made sure the children were available to speak with her.

Her most satisfying moment was when she had her daughter call her Granny on her birthday. It was 8 PM her time, which meant it was past 10 PM Granny's time. My friend felt terrible because she had waited until the end of the day to make the call. But, she could hear Granny say on the phone, "You're the first one who's called today!" Granny repeated it about three times during the phone call.

Activity: When you're ready, send a card or photos to your in-laws. Keep the communication lines open.

<u>The Ex and The Feet</u>

People can say what they want all day long. It is their actions that matter. Stop listening and start watching. Do their actions match their words? If not, watch their feet instead of listening to their words. You are less likely to be surprised or disappointed, and more liable to know what the person is really about when you watch their actions instead of relying on their words. That is watching their feet.

Whether you like it or not, when you have children your ex is a part of your extended family. Watching their feet keeps them honest. Sometimes your ex will say things and then completely forget about it. Follow up the conversation with an email to make it clear what you understood. A text may be enough. Remember, divorce can be a mind-numbing experience, and it can be easy for miscommunications to occur.

There are also times when an ex will say something intentionally to mislead you. Usually, this is an ongoing problem present during the marriage and which will continue forever. In those cases, the ex is pretty well fucked. Keep every conversation by email or text. Save them all. It will be a short matter of time before you can point out to the court that the words do not match the actions. The actions are what matter.

We had a friend whose husband said he wanted every Wednesday night with his three daughters. He insisted on it at court, claiming that he missed his girls and wanted to spend time with them. His words did not match his feet. Once or twice a month, he would cancel his day with his children. Then, he asked the court for more custody to lower the amount of child support he paid. The wife was able to show the court that the husband was not with the children as much as he was already allowed. The court refused his request and told the husband that if he continued to miss the Wednesday nights with the children, they would cancel his visitation for those times and adjust the child support accordingly.

Watch the feet. Don't rely on the words. The path they walk is the true one, and your ex's actions will show you their real intentions.

Note from Leah...

One of my friends was complaining about how her ex said words that didn't match his actions.

"I always support my ex's relationship with the children." Meanwhile...

"I left that relationship behind a long time ago!" Meanwhile...

"Your words go one way, but your feet go another," She remembered telling her ex during the marriage. After the divorce, it wasn't any different. The words didn't match the feet. Fortunately, watching the feet was all that mattered to her, and she didn't put much weight in his words. This kept her from being misled as to what her ex really wanted.

Note from Robin...

One of my friends was extremely disappointed in the actions of her ex upon separation. She tended to be a very honest and trusting person so she believed him when he would tell her that he did this or that. She quickly learned she could no longer trust the person she used to consider her best friend. His actions were completely different from his words. Losing this trust was a hard fact to adjust to after having been in an intimate relationship with a person for so many years.

Activity: Make a list of things your ex says. Write the translation out so you follow the feet and not the words.

Siblings & Parents

Some of you are fortunate to have immediate family that will stand beside you through anything. These may be your siblings, mother, father, and even aunts or uncles. They will be your foundation and help you through the divorce in any way they can. Some will lend emotional support, help watch the kids while you work, or lend money in case your divorce becomes expensive. If you are in this wonderful position, you are blessed. Let them know how much you appreciate their support and return the favor in any way you can.

Some of you will find the opposite. Your family may be opposed to your divorce. They will not support your decision and may even go as far as advocating for your ex instead. This lack of support is a terrible experience that will leave you feeling depressed and abandoned.

Why does this happen? What is it that creates that division in your family? There are a few reasons. One, you could have been wrong about something. You may have been the one who cheated on your spouse in a family that believes strongly in marriage vows. Your family could be very religious and not believe in divorce. You may have put work before family, and you are now facing the consequences of your choice. If that's the case, your best course of action is to change your behavior, do your best, and do better in the future.

Another reason you may not have the support of your family is because of long-standing family issues. A complicated relationship with your parents will not improve with your divorce. Also, if your siblings are competitive or jealous of the past success in your life, they may see the divorce as an opportunity to kick you while you are down. Just because they are family, does not mean they always have your best interests in mind.

There are also cases where your family does not have enough information. You may have kept problems in your marriage secret. Your divorce will come across as rash and unreasonable if they do not know the whole story.

One example is a friend of ours who found out her husband of over fifteen years was gay. Since the husband came from a prominent family with a strong religious background, he pleaded with her to keep his secret even after divorce. In exchange, he gave her everything – custody of the children, alimony, and the bulk of their assets. The woman's husband was a successful businessman, a wonderful father, caring and kind. Her family could not understand the reasons for her divorce. They were hostile towards her and supported her husband. They made the immediate assumption that it must be her fault. She kept her husband's secret for over a decade until her husband felt confident enough to come out of the closet. It was then that her family finally realized what she had gone through and offered her apologies and support.

Note from Leah...

I am fortunate that I had great family support throughout my divorce. I have a close relationship with my family so when the divorce finally occurred it was not a surprise to those family members close to me. I struggled with the decision to divorce for years before actually pulling the trigger. Part of the process to get to this decision was talking with my grandmother. I am very close with my grandmother, and her advice is very dear to me.

Over the years she saw how stressed and upset I was in the relationship and how I had been struggling with this decision. One day we were driving the car home from an outing, and I relayed how sad I was and began to cry. Her response to me was "all I want is to see you happy, and if moving on is what is going to alleviate this stress than that's what I want for you." Her saying this was a great relief for me. I felt as if I had her blessing, not that I needed it, but sometimes in families, it is important to get that support to help you with those hard decisions.

Note from Robin...

My immediate family was divided. Some were supportive, and some were absent. Your parents may have had a high-conflict divorce, and this event can resonate into adult lives. Although I wanted to share the reasons for leaving with some of my family members, but some of them simply did not want to hear it.

Lacking immediate family support hurt more than I think they realized. I can only hope that someday they will be open to hearing the entire story.

Activity: Write a letter to your immediate family, letting them know you appreciate their support.

<u>The Ex's Future Ex</u>

If you have children and your ex remarries, do your best to be on good terms with the new spouse to make your life easier. What this does is allow you to communicate with the new spouse instead of dealing with your ex. Typically it removes a lot of bullshit. It may take a while to be on good terms with your ex's new partner, but it can be done. Be friendly and informative. Your ex has faults (as do you!) and your ex's new partner will find out soon enough what those are. That's why we call them the *Ex's Future Ex.*

We have a friend who absolutely cannot speak to her ex-husband. Whenever issues arose with the children, the conversation would disintegrate into an argument. Arguments weren't good for our friend and definitely not good for the kids. Our friend's ex-husband eventually remarried, and she was surprised to find that she got along with the new wife extremely well. The new wife was aware of her husband's shortcomings and acted as a buffer between the parents. Now, all the child arrangements are between the ex-wife and the new wife.

The Ex's Future Ex can be a great ally. If they have been through a divorce themselves, they understand how the dynamics work and can have great ideas on how to keep things civil. If you want to trade a weekend with your ex, the Future Ex would probably not mind whereas your actual ex would make it into a court event. So stay nice to the Future Ex, this person can help make raising the children easier. And who knows? Maybe sometime in the future, you'll be sharing a drink with the Future Ex, complaining about the ex!

Note from Leah...

Recently, an Ex's Future Ex sent a friend of mine a long-winded email regarding one of her kid's after-school activities. Why didn't she inform them of the schedule? Why was she rescheduling the lessons without their approval? Why was she not letting them know when there was class? She gave a big sigh when she read it. Her ex had just remarried and the after-school activity they were arguing about went back two years. The Ex's Future Ex just joined in on the discussion and sent her the usual complaints from the ex as if they were her own.

My friend understood what was happening here. The ex had probably put his new wife up to it but did not tell the whole story. She took the time to send her a detailed email explaining everything. She stayed kind and civil as she explained. She also attached all the email discussions between the ex and herself from the past two years regarding the after-school activity. It was the ex who had not been informing *her* about schedule changes and the ex who was not letting her know when there was a class. All of the old emails she attached showed that.

She sent the email back, directly to the Future Ex and didn't CC the ex. She never received a reply. Although it would be easy to get mad, my friend mostly felt sad for the Future Ex. She knows what she is going through. She has been there before.

Note from Robin...

I have a good friend who married a man who was previously married with children. She quickly realized that when dealing with the logistics of the shared custody of the children it ran much more smoothly when she eliminated her husband from the equation. Over the years, she and the ex-wife became quite amicable with each other. Everything ran better as a result. They are still friends even though she is now divorced from her husband. She was the Ex's Future Ex in this scenario. Regardless of the role you play, be kind.

Activity: If there's a Future Ex, make a list of kind things to say at the end of each written conversation.

Chapter Three

THE REMODEL

Pretend that you are a house. You are going through a remodel. You know what needs to be worked on. You know what ticks you off and turns you on. You also know what motivates and inspires you. Of course, if you have ever had to remodel a house, you know what a mess that can be. We will start by explaining some of the difficult things that will follow your divorce with some ways in which to handle them. Once the demolition is done, you can work on rebuilding your life the way YOU want.

You're on your way to a new life. Something new is always exciting, the smell of a new car or the feel of new clothes. It gives a feeling of freshness. It's uplifting. Before we get into the remodel, we will need to do a little demolition and review some of the dirty stuff in your divorce. Once we have gone through that, we can discuss how you are going to rebuild your new, incredible life!

The Cold, Hard Truth

Disappointment ~ Criticism ~ Unfriending ~ Anger ~ Sex Stuff

The Cold, Hard Truth can hurt. We originally wanted to title this section "The Yucky Chapter." For a while, we thought of getting rid of this section altogether. But in the end, we realized there was some information that must be shared, even if it hurts.

Not everyone will have what is considered a "high-conflict divorce," that is, a divorce that sees a lot of court action. But, every divorce will have some conflict in it. Disappointment, anxiety, and anger often accompany conflict. What we discuss in this chapter will apply to everyone to some degree or another because everyone experiences conflict at some point in their divorce.

Before you start your new life, you first need to deal with parts of your old life. You need to deal with your expectations, emotional ties, and anger towards your ex and also deal with some mechanical discussions about your body.

Disappointment

Much of our disappointment comes from our expectations of other people. We are disappointed that our ex isn't behaving the way we wanted. We are disappointed that our best friend did not immediately come to help after the ex left. We are disappointed for so many reasons because we expected people to behave or react a certain way. More specifically, we are disappointed that people did not respond the way we wanted them to.

Get used to it.

Being disappointed is like whining, "Why didn't you do it the way *I* wanted you to do it?" Playing the victim is an easy role. Don't play that role. You want the role that gets you on the red carpet, the role of a survivor, a person of strength, and a person of integrity. To play that role, you will need to let go of disappointment.

The easiest way to let go of disappointment is by letting go of expectations. If you have no expectations that the ex is going to remain civil during the divorce, you won't be disappointed by their bad behavior in the courtroom. This is not to say that you will be surprised if you are lucky enough to have a friendly divorce. The truth of the matter is *you don't know what the outcome will be in any given situation so why expect anything?*

Let go of those expectations, and you will no longer be disappointed.

Note from Leah...

In most divorces, disappointment is inevitable. Many of my friends have been extremely disappointed with how an ex has handled things. They did not expect the ex to behave in such a way. There have been incidences of lying, making up things that didn't happen, and hearing stories the ex has told other people that weren't true.

It is hard to imagine a person that was your best friend and confidante for a decade or more suddenly turning on you. This is why we have to write this chapter. It is because it happens more often than not. If you are starting your divorce, you need to change your perspective and lose any expectations. It is always better to expect the worst and be happy when things go better than anticipated.

Note from Robin...

I have a girlfriend who gave me some excellent advice: "You were strong enough to leave him. You're strong enough to take the hits." She was right. Disappointment would come, again and again. You may think, how could a person I lived with for nearly 18 years think that I'm a terrible mother? You may realize that it was not your parenting skills that bothered him... it was the fact that you left. How dare you?

One of my friends had this to say, "I gave up a lot of expectations in marriage, but I had a last one to give up after the divorce. I gave up expecting that my ex would be respectful to me. Giving up this expectation was a tough one. But, the further I got away from that expectation, the less I was disappointed. The hits I was taking after divorce softened. I realized I could not expect my ex to be nice, courteous, or even reasonable. Then, I accepted what I was dealing with, and was better able to handle my divorce."

Activity: Write a list of non-expectations.

Criticism

On the heels of "Disappointment" is "Get Used to Criticism." People are watching you. Yes, they are. You are getting a divorce, or you've just been through one. It's a great thing to talk about. Maybe you are about to have one. Isn't that juicy gossip? Why the divorce? Who left who? Oh, my, and did-you-see-what-she-wore-the-other-day?!

People love to talk. They also love to criticize. Getting divorced brings the critic out in everyone. From "I can't believe he cheated on her" to "Well! She remarried quickly!" the criticism doesn't end in just a few months. The critics will be around for the rest of your life. If you do not think so, look at yourself. Ever talk about someone else's divorce? How long ago was that divorce? Or who they dated? Why they broke up? You can see what we mean.

The best way to handle those sorts of people is not to give them a reason to talk. It will be difficult, but you'll need to put a clamp down on complaining about your divorce. Take the divorce elsewhere like a therapists office or support group, and talk about something else with the critics. Change the conversation into something positive.

One of the critics might be your ex. Your ex may tell everyone what a complete asshole you are. What's worse is that other people are going to believe it. As much as people can behave like adults and know that things are not always black and white, they can't help but want to think there's a bad guy and, especially, a bad ex!

Understand that not everyone will be in your corner, and, to be fair, someone will need to be in your ex's corner. It's ok for your ex to have a fan club. Stay positive and don't bad mouth your ex. Remember to keep the conversation positive and redirect it if you need to. Stay nice to the people in your ex's corner and someday they may realize that you are not the devil incarnate.

Finally, in some of the friendlier divorces, no one will be criticizing you. Actually, we take that back. Someone is criticizing you. YOU! Ease up on yourself. You are your worst critic. Turn off the critic in your head and give yourself a compliment. When you hear yourself self-criticizing, change the conversation! Say compliments to yourself out loud. Move things in a more positive direction.

Note from Leah...

Criticism happens during a divorce, after divorce, and even before the divorce. The criticism may come from outsiders looking in, or it may come from your ex. In my friend's situation, it was occurring before the divorce. Friends would relay complaints he had about something she did or did not do. The criticism behind her back was hurtful. Once separated, she was not surprised that there was further criticism and even completely false comments about what happened.

As a result of criticism in the marriage, she felt that no matter how hard she tried nothing would make her husband happy. After years of trying, she finally realized that her ex had to learn how to make _himself_ happy. What a wake-up call.

Often in marriages, one person looks to the other to fulfill all their needs and make them happy. You cannot make another person happy. They have to learn how to make themselves happy. When you are in a relationship, it is important to remember that you need to compliment one another. When a couple complements one another, they both become the best versions of themselves in that relationship. There is no room for criticism.

Note from Robin...

You will never please your ex. Get used to it. One of my close friends had this to say:

"When I first got divorced, my ex kept making annoying, little comments about things I did. A lot of it was petty stuff: whether my carpets needed cleaning, what the kids had for dinner, who I was with, and where I was going. You'd think we were still married. Since I was married to him for a while, I was used to jumping at his command and fixing things the way he wanted them fixed. Pretty soon, I was driving myself crazy trying to keep up with his demands."

Wait a minute? Didn't she get divorced?

It was then that she realized that he was controlling her, even after divorce. Maybe for him, the marriage was not really over? She was never going to please him. Everything she did was wrong. She was getting nit-picked to death as he attempted to micro-manage her life after they divorced.

For example, when she was at a mediator's office and the mediator asked the ex, "But what is it about *her* that makes you think that she's a bad parent?"

"I'm afraid that all she's giving the kids is chicken nuggets from the microwave," he responded. "I have serious concerns as to whether my children are getting good nutrition."

She looked over at him and thought, "Chicken nuggets? Really? That's what you've got on me?" These were the same chicken nuggets everyone got from the warehouse store. If you were a parent, those chicken nuggets were likely in your freezer.

She got it then. There would be no pleasing him.

Your ex may go around telling everyone in existence that you are a bad parent, ex, and human being. There is no getting around it. Some exes will spread rumors and lies, but your behavior and interaction with people are what will determine what they think of you in the long run. Don't waste breath trying to please the ex. There was a reason you got divorced.

Activity: Write down your ex's name. Next to it write, I am not responsible for his or her happiness.

Unfriend & Block the Ex

You will need a social media remodel. In spite of your best intentions to "remain friends," it may be best not to remain friends or followers on social media. It is too difficult to see an ex moving on, or it may be too difficult for the ex to see that you are. Almost every couple we have talked to has tried to remain connected through social media after their divorce. Almost every time it fails. You are not alone in this.

It's hard to say who pushes the "unfriend" button first. Is it done in a fit of anger? Does the ex just want to disappear? If you were in a long-term marriage, unfriending becomes even more challenging. Everyone can see it. You may have so many friends in common that you won't be able to avoid seeing your ex on social media. You may not be connected directly, but you are connected through your friends and family.

A woman we knew tried to keep her ex on her "friends" list. Unfortunately, her ex left the marriage and went off to "play the field." He would post pictures of the women he was with even though he and his wife had been separated for less than two months. She finally pressed the "unfriend" button.

There may also be some benefits to staying connected on social media, especially if there are kids involved, but as we said previously, this rarely happens. Being connected on social media is like running into your ex every day at the grocery store. It just gets too uncomfortable, and you change stores. In the case of social media, it is easier just to unfriend.

Note from Leah...

Initially, I thought I could remain friends with my ex on social media. We did stay connected for quite some time during the separation. It was mainly to see pictures of our children, but I quickly realized that it was better to cut ties. I was cutting ties with him in all other areas of my life, and social media needed to be a part of that.

With one of my friends, she noticed her ex would make snide remarks about places she had gone or things she was doing. She did not like that he was patrolling. She had this to say: "It took me a while, but I finally pulled the plug and un-friended him. I also took a different approach altogether. I just started using a different social media site. I figured I am re-creating my life and image. Why not start with a new profile to start my new life?"

Note from Robin...

One of my good friends had this to say:
"My ex was never on social media. After we had separated, he was suddenly on there all the time. A picture of me with the kids? Instant acknowledgement from him. A picture of me proudly repairing a faucet in the kitchen? Same thing. I didn't want the ex off my social media initially. I post a lot of kid pictures to share with family. I also felt it was important that he knew what we were up to.

The situation came crashing down later when I visited Manhattan with a boyfriend. The ex knew I was dating. My boyfriend, who had been really good about not posting anything on my site, mentioned he was there with me on social media. Immediately after, I got a message from the ex:

"It's too painful for me to see pictures of you and [boyfriend]... I can no longer see you on social media."

Ok. Lesson learned. She removed the ex from her social media and made sure he couldn't see her either. She let him know that she thought it was for the best. The truth is, she suspected that he had been stalking her online.

There may be resistance to unfriending but, really, it's for the best for everyone.

Activity: Un-friend the ex.

Anger

You will go nowhere with your remodel until you release your anger. Your anger will hold you back. If you put energy into anger, you will not have anything left to build your new life. But you are not alone. *Everyone* has anger when they get divorced. If you think you do not have any anger about your divorce, you are in denial, or you're a part of that .00000001% that had a friendly divorce. Good for you.

No matter who left whom, both people in a divorce will be angry. One is angry because the other one left. The other is angry because the first is not letting go. Do you want to know something cool? The person who lets go of their anger first WINS!

What? Yes. The first person to let go, **wins.**

We knew a guy who let go of his bad marriage and immediately moved on after the divorce was final. He didn't squabble over the money and, in fact, gave his ex more than she was entitled to have. He said, "It was worth it. I hear from friends that she's still complaining about the marriage and the divorce. I let it go, and I'm so much happier because of it." We knew his ex-wife. More than 20 years after the divorce, she is bitter and still complaining about her ex. He moved on, found someone else to love, a new career, and has a great relationship with the rest of the family.

The sooner you release your anger, the sooner you will be able to put things in a better perspective, including seeing your ex in a way you never did before. Once you release your anger, you might have empathy towards your ex. Besides, once you let go of all those angry feelings, you will feel so much better.

How do you release anger? Part of it is time, and part of it is the mental effort. We included some of our experiences to share, along with an activity that can make releasing your anger easier.

Note from Leah...

The anger sneaks up on you at different times. In the beginning, it is very present, but as time goes on it will lessen. There will also be times where you think that "wow, I think I'm finally getting over this" and then BAM, something re-ignites it. Anger is normal, and various things can initiate feelings that you may not be acknowledging. It does not serve you to suppress your feelings.

If you continue to suppress your anger, your body will respond to it in other ways, through illness or aches and pains. I had a friend who woke up one morning with a really bad urinary tract infection. This surprised her because she had never had one before and was surprised at the pain she was experiencing. She called the doctor and scheduled an appointment immediately.

Simultaneously, she looked up the emotional meaning of anger and to her surprise saw a UTI can be a result of being pissed off. She thought back to her previous day and recalled a conversation with her ex that made her mad. She was harboring anger and not realizing it. But her body did, and it told her.

The moral of this story is this: listen to your body. It will notify you when your mind is distracted. Once she realized this and was able to: acknowledge it, release the anger, and forgive; poof, the UTI was gone. I am amazed at the ability we have to heal ourselves.

Note from Robin:

One of my childhood friends had been given a unique Christmas ornament one year. To the giver, it represented clarity, truth, and a new beginning. It sounds sweet, doesn't it? Whenever my friend looked at that ornament, it reminded her of deception, disloyalty, and pain. To her, the Christmas ornament told her that she had been lied to in her marriage.

For nearly ten years after the husband bought that ornament, she helped put it on the tree each Christmas. The first Christmas after she separated from him, she took a hammer and smashed that ornament to pieces. She felt a sudden release of nearly ten years of pain and humiliation. It was a symbolic act and one that helped her feel free.

Activity: Your relationship broke. It's true. It broke and will not get fixed. Break something. A vase. A plate. A diet. Find something in your house that you can break, or buy something cheap to break. Take a hammer to it. Smash it up. Get the anger out. You will feel better afterward.

Sex Stuff

Once you have left your ex (or your ex has left you), it is time to get tested. Immediately. Even if you think that your ex never, ever, ever would sleep with anyone but you during marriage heed this warning - your ex may have cheated. Cheating does not always have to do with the health of the relationship, although that can be a factor. Sometimes, cheaters just cheat. On top of that, they are not always found out. Monogamy is great. Monogamy is wonderful. Monogamy just doesn't work for some people.

When you start dating, continue to get tested regularly. It is naive to assume that a person is completely honest with you about their past sexual history. People will lie. Be safe. Get tested.

One woman we knew went back and forth with her ex after they were separated. Her ex swore he was faithful in the marriage even though she had proof otherwise. She kept sleeping with him on and off while they were trying to "work things out." She ended up with a venereal disease that she now has to disclose to future sex partners. She was exclusive with her ex, but he still claims that the STD did not come from him.

Using a condom is absolutely necessary, but they do not always work. There will always be guys who don't want to wear one. If you are a woman, remember to stick to your guns – no condom, no sex. You've been married. You've had sex. You know you can get yourself off if you need to. Sex is optional. A condom is not.

Condoms are now available online with two-day shipping.

Note from Leah...

Even after your first test post-marriage, continue to get tested regularly. This should *always* be the case. I have seen many girlfriends who thought they were in committed marriages or relationships only to find out that their partner cheated on them and did not have the sense to wear a condom.

Note from Robin...

Don't wait to get tested. It can be scary, humiliating, and embarrassing to do so. Fortunately for me, my doctor automatically recommended I get one after I had explained I'd gotten divorced. This saved me the embarrassment of asking for it myself.

Activity: Get tested.

New Life, New Space

Eliminate Clutter ~ Downsize ~ Paint, Soaps & Sundries

Your new life is going to have some new space in it. You could be moving into a new place, or you may have extra space in your home since your ex left. For those of you with children, if you are the person that is moving out of the family home and into a new place, it is important to set up the kid's room first. They are going to be having a hard time understanding what is happening, depending on their age. Having their new room set up with familiar things will help them transition more smoothly. We have included several ways to enjoy and transition into your new space. Celebrate it!

Eliminate Clutter

Your new life has no room for clutter. This goes for your mind, as well. Clutter that piles up in your mind will make it difficult for you to think clearly. It's time to take inventory of your house and your mind. This will help you create your new life and new space.

First, eliminate clutter in your home. Clutter piles up and gets in the way of everyday living. It has a way of accumulating in corners and on counter-tops. The items you need might be in a pile of clutter instead of in their proper place. Clutter makes it difficult for you to find things quickly. It takes time to find things in clutter and time is simply something you do not have a lot of right now.

Take a small pile of clutter each day and put it away. You can also store a few extra items each time you visit a room. Make hard decisions on whether or not you need certain items. The more things you have, the more time you spend taking care of those things. With the free space in your home, you will be able to add things that are useful and healthy. Space in your home can be filled with a plant or a comfortable chair. You may want to keep the space empty and just revel in the freedom of the space.

One of the men we were talking with had moved to a new place after the divorce. He used the move to eliminate clutter. He got into the habit of asking himself if he needed the stuff he had. He continually finds ways to keep things off the countertops and goes through his "junk drawer" at

LEAH SCOTT & ROBIN SASSI

least once a month. His ulterior motive, "I don't like to dust, and I don't want to pay for maid service."

Next, it's time to de-clutter your mind. Your mind will benefit from the free space, too. Getting rid of the mental clutter that takes up energy will give you the time to think about things that matter. You will find that you are more productive, better focused, and more relaxed. Take an inventory of the things you have no more time for and use meditation techniques to remove them from your mind. Remember, the more you hold on to, the more time you spend thinking about those things. It is wasted time.

Note from Leah...

The process of de-cluttering is an ongoing event. I have lived in my new place for a year, and I am amazed at how quickly clutter happens. It is a continuous effort to stay on top of it. I have realized that I do not need three sets of baking dishes in the same size or various sets of wine glasses. I started small by donating items that I no longer needed. It feels good to let go of stuff because, really, that is all it is - just stuff.

If you are still in the home you shared with your ex, it is time to get rid of your shared life, including pictures, plants or artwork. If they have negative memories attached, then it is okay to get rid of them. De-cluttering will release you from old habits and help you to move on.

Note from Robin...

Clutter happens. It sneaks up in my house in unexpected places. Individual drawers or cabinets end up being clutter spaces. They hold all of the things I cannot find a place for.

At some point in time, I go through the clutter and throw things out. It is amazing how many things I've held onto that I don't need.

After de-cluttering, I feel better mentally. It's as if I threw away the clutter in my mind. Now, I am free to think of other things!

Activity: Start with one drawer and clean it out. Just do one drawer at a time. Before you know it your home will be de-cluttered, and so will your mind.

<u>Downsize</u>

Downsizing is difficult for some people because they look at it as a step down financially. Everyone seems to want bigger and better – a new house, faster car, more modern appliances. Bigger is NOT better in this case. You and your ex have just divided a household. Downsize accordingly.

If you rent, the most efficient way to downsize is to get a smaller place. If you have kids, you may feel like you need the same amount of space as before. This is untrue. You will be child sharing with your ex, so your space will only be used part of the time. You won't need the extra office, man-cave, or closet space. If you have two kids, they can share a room. What matters is how much you love the kids, not the things you give them or the fact that they have their own room.

You can downsize in the kitchen too, especially when it comes to food. Cookies. So good. So fattening. But do you really need to bake three dozen? Did you know you could store the cookie dough in the freezer? Yup! Then you can just take some out when you need it. Casseroles are easy, but you are cooking for fewer people now. The extras can also go in the freezer. The freezer is your friend, and you will save a ton of money by wasting less.

Little by little, you will come to realize how much time, space, and expense your ex took up. There will be some adjustments. But, you will find that the soap you buy lasts longer, your sink doesn't need to be cleaned as often, and a smaller coffee pot is ok. Your sheets will stay clean longer, and you can take up the whole bed. Downsizing will help you save money, simplify your life, and reduce stress.

Note from Leah...

As I thought about moving out of the house that I shared with my ex, I went through different emotions and phases. The idea of downsizing initially scared me. "But I need a same sized house! I have boys!" is what I told my good friend. I honestly believed that I did at that moment too. But I didn't. At that moment I believed it, but I was wrong. I didn't need a big house or that much space. I just needed a place that I could make my own – a home for my boys. It is hard to break old habits but, as time went on, I realized that I would be just fine in a smaller home.

As a result of downsizing, I was able to de-clutter and purchase new things. This was the fun part. It felt good to free myself from old things that no longer served a purpose in my life. I had fun decorating my home how I *liked* for the first time in a decade. It was a time for transformation and a fresh start, and my favorite part is that when my friends come by, they say "this house is just like you." Mission accomplished. I created my home and sanctuary

Note from Robin...

Downsizing was difficult for me. I'm a warehouse club shopper. I like my gallon jug of pickles. The thing is, I don't like pickles. But, when I was married, I had to buy them. I don't need two loaves of bread anymore. I don't make sandwiches. I don't need those big blocks of cheese. Cheese makes me fat. (I DO need all that closet space, though.)

Since I owned my place, moving wasn't an option considering the real estate market at the time. Instead, I converted a loft area that my ex and I had shared as an office and moved a nanny in there instead. I saved on child-care AND had the advantage having someone to help with the housework.

Activity: Assess your home and belongings. What is no longer serving you at this phase in your life? It is okay to purge. Have a yard sale or donate. Shed things from your life that no longer serve a purpose.

<u>Paint, Soaps, and Sundries</u>

Now that you've downsized and de-cluttered, your new space is almost ready. Because of the divorce, you are now able to make choices about big things such as where you live and how you spend your free time. Those things matter, but it's the little things that will resonate with you every day. When you were married, you made concessions on these little things. You may have bought soaps your partner liked, toothpaste that you both agreed on, and coffee when you preferred tea. After the divorce, you may still be in the habit of buying those little things.

When you're ready to change these little things out, you'll find items that work better for you. They will go a long way towards making your space your own. These are the inexpensive items that you need to buy anyway. For example, you may like soaps that are scented or not. You may have a preference for vanilla coffee beans instead of espresso. You like white bread, but your ex always bought wheat.

Now is the time to make adjustments towards the little things that YOU like. If you've come out of a long marriage, you might not know what these are. If that's the case, break out of the habit of buying the same thing and try something new. You may find new things you love that you would not have tried before.

Good energy matters. If you're still in the place you shared with your ex, it's now time to paint. All the bad energy and arguments with your ex have seeped into all aspects of your life, including the walls! Bad energy from your last relationship lingers in the things around you. You can burn sage in the house all you want, but sometimes a good coat of paint is all you need.

If you do it yourself, painting doesn't have to be expensive. Take a weekend that you don't have the kids and paint your place. Repainting can be a particularly satisfying experience. With each stroke of the roller, think, "I am painting over the past and getting ready for the future."

If painting the entire place seems too big a task, start with a small space like the bathroom. Pick colors that you identify with, or that soothe you. Move pictures around in your home to go with the new color. The change will feel fantastic. So go to the store, pick out some paint, and do it yourself! Your place will look better, and you will feel fresh and renewed.

Note from Leah...

There are many ways to change the energy in your home. A fresh, new coat of paint is a great way. You get to choose whatever color you want. No more compromising! It's your wall, your paint color, and your home!

When it comes to soaps, and body wash, and scrubs there is an abundance of choices. Spoil yourself! Choose what you like, and you will smell and feel delightful.

Note from Robin...

When I was married, everything in my house was white, white, white. The decor was minimal, and there was barely anything on the walls. Items on surfaces were highly discouraged. After I divorced, I started redecorating by painting my baseboards and then looked at the grand piano in the corner. I put the piano lid down and added pictures of the kids, decorative flowers, and eventually a fishbowl with a beautiful Japanese fighting fish. Then, I added my art easel in the corner. Making the space "mine" was a satisfying experience.

A friend of mine also explained it like this:

"My ex didn't like the soaps I picked out. I did most of the shopping, so he would request I buy different soap. He didn't like the pink ones, but I did. They were gentler on my skin. We settled on a soap in between. It was green, not pink, and smelled good. Now, I'm a soap aficionado. I'm not just picking the pink soaps in bulk at the warehouse store. I'm buying the fancy, specialty, wrapped, handmade soaps at boutiques."

Take stock of your soaps. Are they the ones YOU want? Or the ones the ex wanted you to buy? This is the time for YOU!

Activity: Buy a new soap, scrub or lotion. Try something new!

New Life, New You

Enjoy New Things, New Experiences ~ Dress Well ~ Shoes ~ The Muff

Your remodel also calls for a personal makeover. The makeover doesn't have to be drastic or expensive. You can take incremental steps toward the new you. You're on your way towards becoming your own person, and this may take a bit of exploration. Try something new and if it doesn't work, try something else. The point is to find what works for YOU, not what you think would please another person.

We will start by setting you up to enjoy new things and new experiences along with a few recommendations to remodel yourself. Afterward, you can continue with a confident new you!

Enjoy New Things, New Experiences

Creating a new you will be easy once you are open to the change. Your old relationship may have left you in a rut. If you were in a long relationship, you likely had a routine for everything. You and your ex established these routines as a part of being a couple. We cannot help it. The people we are with shape how we conduct our day-to-day activities. While routines are good, it's time to shake things up.

The first step towards creating your new life is by enjoying new things and new experiences. You are creating your new life. Being open to new experiences and people is a great way to start. New experiences mean new routines and new activities to teach you to enjoy what you haven't experienced before. Have some fun with it!

A mutual friend of ours recently got out of a marriage with a guy who liked to stay at home. Their relationship centered around meals at home with a movie. After the divorce, she wanted to try something new. The idea of staying in and watching movies was no longer appealing to her. She started by taking her bike out for a ride every day. After about a year, we were surprised to find that she became a very dedicated cyclist. Each weekend, she goes out with a group and has widened her social circle as a bonus. She has all the gear that she added little by little, including an amazing new bicycle. We would never have thought that she would become a cyclist. In opening herself up to new things and new experiences, she found something that she enjoyed.

It's time to go out of your comfort zone a bit. You don't have to go parachute diving or take a trip to the Amazon unless that's really your thing. It can be as simple as taking a different road home. You can try different restaurants and socialize with groups that you and your ex didn't socialize with. A small new experience can open the door to many more things.

As you begin to branch out, you'll become bolder. Mistakes will be made, but that's ok. Perhaps skydiving wasn't a good idea. But, you'll never know unless you try. So, give new things, new experiences, and even new people a shot. You may find an adventurous part of yourself that you never knew existed!

Note from Leah…

New things and new experiences present themselves in many different ways. It can be going to new restaurants with your friends for unfamiliar, exotic food. Maybe it's chatting with a new person who doesn't match the description in your head of 'your type.' Whatever it may be, stay open-minded to new experiences. You never know what friendships will come out of it. As for skydiving, I recently met a person that loves skydiving. His Zen is jumping out of a plane and feeling like he's flying. You don't know until you try.

Note from Robin…

I remember the first time I went grocery shopping after my ex left the house. I suddenly thought, "I don't have to buy that stupid cheese anymore!" As I went down the next aisle, I realized I didn't need to buy the stupid bread, stupid beer, or stupid canned sausages either. My entire shopping cart was different! It was a *smart* shopping cart. Yes. Grocery shopping became a new experience.

After I got further out of my old relationship, I also found a new love of travel. For about a year after my divorce finalized, I found myself on a plane visiting new places almost every month. There were definite advantages to shared custody! I no longer had to ask permission or arrange for child-care while I was gone. I met people throughout the world and got to explore cities I never explored before.

Activity: Make a list of things that you have thought about trying but never felt you had the time for. It could be a new type of food, class, or social group.

<u>Dress Well</u>

Dressing well doesn't have to be expensive, but you do need to put some effort into it. Take the time to keep your clothes in good shape. Find the one piece that you can add to your wardrobe that will help you create three more outfits. Sometimes it's as simple as adding a new pair of pants.

One great reason to dress well is that you might run into the ex at any time. The ex can pop up anywhere: the grocery store, the gym, or driving down the street. You were a couple for some time. It's likely that you travel some of the same roads together, know some of the same people, or live in the same town. If you have kids, you'll run into your ex frequently. How do you want to look when you run into your ex? Do you want to look ragged and run-down? Do you want to look amazing?

That's what we thought.

It's so easy to get lazy when it comes to looking good. Hair gets shaggy. Clothes get sloppy. You think, "It's just a quick trip to the grocery store! Who could I possibly run into?" as you throw on that ratty t-shirt and flip-flops.

Please. Stop. Think. "What if I ran into my ex right now? Would I want to look like this?" If not, change what you're wearing and put on your sexy attitude. You never know who you're going to run into at the grocery store... including your EX!

Note from Leah...

Dressing well is a good habit to get into overall. Remember, you're creating a new life, a new image, a new you. It's time to look fabulous. Enjoy re-creating your image. You will shine, and everyone will notice.

In the first six months of the divorce while I was re-creating my new life and image I was on a work trip with people whom I had not seen in over a year. I had several people come up to me and say, "Wow, you look different" and "You look fabulous! You're glowing!" I didn't have the nerve to say "Hell yeah, cause I'm free and happy" but I was definitely thinking it.

Note from Robin...

One morning I got up and didn't have any pressing appointments that day. Even so, I wanted to wear a particular shirt. The shirt only went with a particular skirt, which only went with a pair of heels. The next thing I knew, I was dressed pretty nice for nothing in particular.

Later that day, I went to pick up my daughter from school. My ex wasn't there, but for some reason, my ex's new *wife* was there! I didn't look frantic, or sloppy. I felt good that I was dressed well.

Activity: Reorganize your closet. Have all your favorite pieces of clothing easily accessible.

<u>Shoes</u>

For anyone, good quality shoes are a great investment and an incredible ego boost. Now that your shoe size isn't changing every six months like in elementary school, it makes sense to invest in quality shoes that you will wear for a decade. You can *feel* the difference.

If you're hesitant about investing your money in a pair of shoes, let's put it into perspective: You pay $100 for a pair of shoes. You wear them once a week for two years. This means you wore the shoes 104 times. Every time you wore the shoes, it cost you 96¢. By amortizing your shoes, you can see how much it costs to dress yourself each day. For example, if you do the same thing with a shirt, that $20 shirt worn once a week for one year only cost you 38¢ each time you wore it! You could have clothes that are amortized down to 5¢ a day. What a bargain!

Check out the stores when they have sales. Go to an outlet store or stock up at the end of the year blowouts. You can find incredibly good deals on quality shoes that go well with many outfits. Dressing up a little also helps to fight any depression or blows to your ego after a divorce. Live a little and recognize the long-term monetary investment of quality shoes. Buy them and wear them. You'll feel great from head to toe!

Note from Leah...

"Life is short, wear cute shoes." I have this sign in my closet as a reminder to wear cute shoes but, I will be honest, I have a bit of a problem when it comes to shoes. I love them. I have lots. I also know that I am not the exception when it comes to women and shoes, and even some men are like this. Invest in shoes that you love and buy various versions, flats, heels, and some really sexy ones. I guarantee when you wear sexy shoes, you can't help but radiate sexiness as a result!

Note from Robin...

When I talk to old women, one of the most common remarks I hear is, "I wish I could still wear heels." After I had got divorced, I realized that I had very few heels, aside from the one or two pairs for formal occasions. Time was ticking. I realized that I could become one of those old women who say, "I wish I could still wear heels." I immediately went on a shoe-buying spree. I was determined not to live with regret! I bought a pair of heels a month for about a year, and now I have several to choose from. That way, when I'm older, I can say, "Damn, I wore heels and rocked that shit."

Activity: Make a list of your top five outfits. Be detailed. Include clothes, shoes, makeup, hair. Now you have your top five outfits ready for future dates. You're welcome!

Update the Muff

The muff is the hairy region of the anatomy, above the legs but below the tummy. You know what we mean. We could write a whole book on the history of the muff. For a long time in history, the muff was free-flowing, hairy, unshaven, and completely natural. Then, someone got the bright idea to start trimming... or shaving.... or whatever. This soon progressed to waxing.

The muff waxing has gone through many variations. Early on, it was a simple cleanup of excess stray hairs. Then, the remaining hair became less and less. There was a time when the "landing strip" was popular for women. It was a simple straight line of hair, supposedly to guide males to the right area – in case they needed any help with navigation. Then, there were the heart-shaped muff and the completely bald muff. There were Brazilians, manzilians, bleaching, and anus waxing!

At the time of this writing, the hairy muff is making a comeback. It may be outdated to have the landing strip muff or the completely bald muff. Since you have been out of circulation for a while, it might be advisable to take a look at some media materials to see what is the preferred muff-scaping of the moment. It's always nice to be in fashion – even down there!

Men. If you are reading this, this goes for you too. Manscaping is mandatory. Take an inventory of other parts of your body while you're at it. Are you sporting a lower back fluffy rug? Time to take that off. Got a patch of caveman hair between the shoulder blades? Take that off, too. You can shave or trim those sensitive lower areas yourself. You'll find that you look more appealing naked, with the additional advantage of looking much more robust when aroused.

Note from Leah...

This is a must for both men and women. Men, if you haven't done this yet, you are the exception to the norm. Learn how to Manscape. Women will be thankful.

Note from Robin...

I love a man with a properly maintained muff area. The overall feel is fantastic. Added to that, I appreciate a man who takes the time to groom just for me.

Activity: We think you know what to do here.

New Problems, New Strategy

Document ~ Insurance ~ Legal Stuff ~ Passwords

In an ideal would, people could get divorced without going to court. Unfortunately, not only is getting a divorce emotionally devastating but getting a divorce also throws ordinary people into a situation they are completely unprepared for mentally and financially.

This section is not about legal advice. This is life advice. This is about covering your ass and keeping your cool. We share the tricks we learned *and* the stuff we wish we knew about before getting divorced.

<u>Document</u>

This is the most valuable piece of information you will receive: *Document everything.*

You will be surprised by how much your ex's memory changes after separating. All of a sudden you will hear through mutual friends about how YOU never did any housework, how YOU never watched the kids, and how YOU cheated in the relationship. You will be portrayed as the "bad ex," for the simple reason that some people need a bad guy to blame when a relationship fails.

Your ex may need to think that they have been wronged, and may point to you as the bad guy. There is no bad guy. You know that. But, you still need to protect yourself when someone says you are. Your ex will fabricate events that never happened. This is where documenting comes in. Keep records of the dates the children are with you. When couples separate, they rarely have anything laid out or agreed upon when it comes to child sharing. You are not writing for the ex. You are writing for the judge who is going to see it, the parenting evaluator who will determine who your children live with, and possibly even for law enforcement.

You will save every email, text message, and voice mail between you and your ex. Every time YOU send an email, text message, or leave a voice mail, imagine that a judge in family court is watching you. Doing this will keep you from saying stupid stuff like, "How could you do such a thing! You make me want to kill you!" <u>That</u> statement will be put to the court by your ex as, "Your honor, she said, and I quote, '[I] want to kill you!' Therefore, I fear for my life and the safety of the children, which is why I should get total custody, the house, the car, all the retirement money, and a restraining order."

Keep your cool and keep your tone civil. Your ex will be frustrated beyond belief at your apparent disengagement and analytical approach to everything. If you're lucky, your ex will lose his or her cool and send a scathing email to you, and sound unreasonable, emotional, and altogether unbalanced.

You may be the fortunate exception to the rule by having one of those divorces where everything goes well, but life is not a fairy tale, and people *can* get nasty when it comes to money and children. Document everything.

Note from Leah...

This is advice I consistently received from those already on this journey. It is so important to document everything in writing in some way or another. Once you separate from your ex, the communication gets quite blurry. Emotions are involved, and information becomes distorted. It's time to cover your ass. Document.

Note from Robin...

If there were only one piece of advice I could give a person getting divorced, it would be to *document everything*. I learned this through a very good friend of mine who had this experience:

"When I separated from my ex, I told him he could see the children or have them whenever he wanted. He came up with the schedule. He canceled times to be at work, take vacations, or spend time with friends. I kept track of the times and percentages with each parent on a handy spreadsheet I created.

When we finally got to mediation, my ex only had the kids about 28% of the time. I had documented everything, and it helped. I think he sincerely believed with all his heart that he was with the kids 50% of the time. It was just like our marriage.

My ex left a trail of emails showing his attempts to control every aspect of my life. Properly saved, printed and presented in court was the best validation that I am better off without that asshole."

Activity: Create a spreadsheet and file folder on your computer and start keeping all your documents in one place. You will be thankful when you need to reference in the future.

Insurance

Insurance comes in a variety of forms. Life insurance is one of them. Stashing cash is another. The moment you move out or separate, or even anticipate doing so, open a separate bank account because it's highly likely things are going to get ugly with finances. The ex may play nice in the beginning, but that won't last. You want to know that *your* money is not going to be drained one day by your ex.

Things will get ugly no matter how much you think, "they would *never* act or treat me that way." They will! Of course, there are cases where people have a very amicable divorce, and if that is your case, that's awesome! Seriously. But that's the exception and not the rule. Not to say that you're not exceptional. It's just that amicable break-ups rarely happen. The norm we've found is that "amicable" is not the norm. Stash away some emergency cash as insurance. It's smart to do even if you're not going through a divorce!

The other insurance you should have is life insurance. If you already have it, make sure you update your beneficiaries immediately. One person we knew didn't. We knew this woman whose husband died of cancer. They had three kids together. She was a beautiful woman, and her children were charming and polite. A few years after the husband passed away, she found love again and married a man who was divorced from his wife and had two kids. His ex-wife lived down the street. After a few months of marriage, the new husband died of a sudden heart attack. The wife was devastated. The ex-wife was thrilled. It turned out the guy had not changed the beneficiary to his life insurance policy, so all of it went to his ex-wife.

Courts often ask parents to get life insurance to replace child support in case one parent dies. For example, parents may be asked to secure a life insurance policy amounting to $100,000.00 in case either of them pass away. However, the money doesn't need to go to the ex. An allocated amount can go to the purpose of supporting the children, and the remaining amount can go to whoever you want. In fact, you can set up a trust, so the money is controlled or monitored by a third party. That way, you know the money is being used for your children and not for your ex.

Changing beneficiaries should be at the top of your to-do list after leaving your ex. It's important to be proactive in such situations. You are on your own now, doing your own finances, managing your own assets. We understand that this may be an entirely new role for you. It could be that your ex handled all these responsibilities. If that is the case, then it is time for you to get smart with your finances by changing your beneficiaries, opening new bank accounts, learning how to invest, and stashing cash. This is another part of your life where you get to hit 'refresh.'

Note from Leah...

This is the tidbit of advice I received from every person I knew divorcing. Stash some cash away, even if it's a small amount. It comes in handy in the future to have for little things here and there. You have no idea what the future holds and how good or bad things may get so having some extra cash on hand is a necessity.

Right after separating, a mediator told me that it was time to redo my will and living trust. Great idea, especially if you have kids. If your ex is in control of your advance health care directive, someone else would be a better choice to act in your best interests. Change that right away.

Note from Robin...

Stashing cash is a concept I wish I had known about when I first divorced. My divorce was initially inexpensive. However, a year after it was finalized, I was still paying for ongoing legal costs. I spent nearly two years in a difficult financial situation, with no savings, no cash, and a case that never seemed to end. Having some cash stashed would have relieved a lot of stress.

As for my life insurance, I changed that right away. There was no way I was going to leave it to my ex!

Activity: Download a list of financial and legal things to be done when getting a divorce. Make sure changing beneficiaries is the first. Start saving cash today.

<u>Legal Stuff</u>

There are many options out there for legal assistance. If you're not able to hire an attorney, there are resources within the court system to help you. Some courts have family law seminars or assistance centers to help with forms. There are also classes that explain the various steps in obtaining a divorce and costs associated. Most of this information is located on family court websites, so check out a class or make an appointment to get legal help. Don't feel that you don't have the money or the resources to take care of this because you do. There are resources out there. Make sure to utilize them!

The family court websites are not the only place with information. There are also a lot of resources you can find by doing a simple online search. Child support calculators are available in most states, but the laws are different depending on where you are. These websites can also calculate spousal support.

Do as much research as you can online. There's a ton of free information out there that can save you money. Before you waste money asking your attorney, learn a little online about what your rights are. You may discover that what you want is impossible or expensive. Or you may find that you have more rights than you ever imagined. Type in your questions and do some of the legwork yourself.

A friend of ours did just that and nearly fainted when she saw how much her ex was supposed to be assisting her. She had been struggling financially, and he kept making comments that he was helping her enough. These were empty threats. Our friend ended up using a paralegal to help her with her divorce and got what she deserved.

If you're ready to get an attorney, your best option is to get referrals from friends. When you do start searching, don't just go with the first one you call. They will be working for you so make sure you have a list of questions to ask them that will pertain to your case, a ballpark estimate of how long everything will take, and the approximate cost. Obviously, shit happens, and things typically take much longer when the court system is involved, so be mentally prepared for delays.

Note from Leah...

When is it the right time to get an attorney? It depends on your situation. For example, a friend of mine had this situation:

"I initially thought that it would be a simple process, since we didn't have many assets together, and had worked out the child custody on our own. My ex even recommended a mediator. I was excited that we were able to keep it amicable and keep the costs low.

The mediator appointment never happened, and things quickly went downhill. The saying "once the rings come off, the gloves come on" is, unfortunately, a true one."

For the people recently divorced who I have met, it is more often that they had a difficult divorce rather than friendly one. Be prepared to get an attorney. I was fortunate enough that my company offered legal insurance. It's a monthly fee taken out of your check with your other benefits. The amount covered depends on the insurance plan. It's worth looking into for your divorce and for other legal questions you might have.

I heard that people tend to choose attorney's who are similar to them in demeanor. This happened to be true in my case. For example, the attorney I chose is well respected and has been in business for 20 years. She is calm, collected and doesn't get rattled. Be choosy with who you choose! You want to get what you're rightfully owed from the marriage, but choosing the wrong attorney will just waste your money.

Note from Robin...

The internet has a lot of information on divorce. When I first got divorced, I didn't do too much research. After a while, I learned so much about family law. Not only did I learn about attorneys and child support, I learned about parenting coordinators, guardians ad litem, forensic psychologists, and vocational evaluators. I could even look up court decisions regarding issues that I was currently facing to see how law played out.

Activity: Write a list of specific legal questions you need answered. Do some preliminary research. If you do hire an attorney or paralegal, the information you find will help you to ask specific questions to get the answers you need.

Passwords

It's time to come up with new passwords. The strategy here is to protect your privacy. Do not rely on the old passwords you used with your ex. If you were the one who left a high-conflict relationship, there's a good possibility you will get hacked by your ex. This means that the ex will go into your email, snoop through your text messages, view your photos, and see who it is you're interacting with on social media. Changing your passwords will help keep your divorce from escalating by ensuring that your private life remains private.

Changing your passwords also brings us to getting your ex off your phone plan or you off of theirs. As soon as possible, this needs to be separate. Your ex doesn't need access to the numbers you call or that call you. We knew a woman whose ex had access to the calls she made on her phone. He called every number to find out whose number it was and what that person had to do with his wife. Sadly, many of the numbers were business clients. She eventually canceled her service and simply got a new phone and number.

Here is a short list of some of the passwords you will need to change:

1. Bank Accounts
2. Phone
3. Computer
4. Online shopping sites
5. Online movie streaming
6. Email
7. Social Media

Note from Leah...

I recently learned a lesson here. I accidently dropped my phone in the toilet. Yes. It was in my back pocket and thank God it was at my friend's house and not a public restroom! Anyhow, in the less than five seconds it was in the toilet (yes, it was clean) I thought I was all in the clear. However, a couple of hours later when the screen started warping I knew I was in trouble.

Twenty-four hours later of burying my phone in rice and it still wasn't better. I took it to a shop to get fixed and thank goodness it was only in need of a new screen. The lesson learned from this experience was that as I was trying to figure out what back-ups were in the cloud, I realized my ex had set this up. It was the first time I had even gone to the site. It was automatically synching all contacts, so at anytime he could have had access since he created the passwords on my behalf!

I didn't have my photos backed up to the cloud, but you can see how this could potentially be a problem, especially if you have kids and especially if online people sporadically send you intimate photos. The moral of this story is make sure you log in to all your electronic devices and change the passwords, including ipads, phones, icloud, etc. It's a precautionary measure to protect your privacy.

Note from Robin...

"Hello! Phone company, how may I help you?"

"Yes! I'd like to take [insert name] off my phone plan," I replied.

"Ok! Is there any reason for the change?"

"Yes," I said. "We are getting divorced."

"Oh no! I'm so sorry..."

"I'm not! I'm glad it's happening!"

"Oh..." [pause] "Then... congratulations...?"

"Damn straight!"

laughter

Activity: Make a list of all your electronic devices, especially those synched to the cloud. Change the passwords today.

New Challenges, New Resources

Third Party Support ~ Family & Friends ~ Enhance Basic Skills

You're going to face challenges that you've never faced before, and you will face many of them alone. No one will be able to go through your divorce for you. Some of the challenges you face will be because of children, the legal system, or from living on your own for the first time in years. This does not mean that you cannot rely on others to help.

When facing these new challenges, use all available resources. It can be difficult for people to rely on others during divorce. Relying on others is not a weakness. When done in a healthy, independent way, it is an exercise in trust. During the marriage, you may have done it all -- worked full-time, cared for the kids, and taken care of the household tasks. But divorce is another full-time job. For a time, you will need extra help, and this is where you will need to learn to rely on others.

Third Party Support.

Third party support is support you have to pay for. It involves engaging professionals for childcare, housekeeping, and book-keeping. It could be lawn care for the home if your ex was the one who used to do it. It can be online ordering for groceries or household supplies. It can be a personal assistant to manage your social calendar. If you're able to afford these services, they can help you transition into your new life and free up your time so you can get through your divorce.

One of the new challenges you may face is finding a new job or working hours different from what you were used to previously. As a result, you may have to seek childcare. There are many options out there, from home daycare providers to larger, corporate ones. The range in price is wide with differences from region to region. Some cities have overnight daycare for parents who work the night shift. Children can drop in and sleep in a safe environment with a responsible person supervising. This is an excellent resource for nurses, police officers, and others who suddenly find themselves as a single parent with a demanding job.

Third party support can also be a cleaning service that comes in once a week or even once a month. No one may clean your house as you do, but having an extra hand will save you the time you need for something else. It may also help reduce stress. If you don't have a chance to shop, you can order your groceries online. Your third party support does not have to be an in-person professional.

Call in lawn service, get in touch with the handyman to fix the washer, and rely on the professionals that can help make your life easier. Third party support is an excellent resource to help get through the challenges your new life will bring.

Note from Leah...

At my wedding, a very good friend said while toasting "Hire a maid. It's cheaper than therapy." This comment received a big laugh from the guests. However, it *is* really good advice. It is hard for one person to keep up with taking care of a home, kids, job, etc... You get my point. I hired a housecleaner to come as often as I could afford. It alleviated the resentment of feeling like I was doing it all.

As a working mother, it was imperative I hire help, specifically a housecleaner and daycare for my children. I was fortunate to find a fabulous home daycare when they were babies. The caretaker I found was the most caring woman, and I knew my boys were being loved while I was away. However, as they got a bit older, I decided to transition them to a larger daycare center. The socialization was perfect for them, and so was the structure. Go with what feels right and know that your child typically stops crying within seconds after you leave.

Note from Robin...

People have often asked me how I can "do it all." The simple truth is that I don't. I'm a master at delegating certain tasks to free myself up for more important ones. I balance out the cost by making sure I'm productive during the time I'm employing help. If someone is cleaning my house, I'm not socializing or sleeping. I am working.

I've had cleaning service off and on throughout my adult life. I use it when I need it. If I'm particularly busy, I will rely on it more. If I have the time, I will do it myself. The key is to balance when you need it and when you don't.

Activity: Review your to-do list. What can a third party handle?

<u>Family and Friends.</u>

Don't be shy accepting help from family and friends. They are an excellent resource. They love you and want to help you get through the challenges you're facing. Chances are, some of them have gone through it before and will just 'get it,' so take them up on their offers to watch the kids so you can run errands or go out with friends. Little things like this will help you during this hard time.

You may have your pride and think that you can adjust to your new life without any help. This is untrue. You may need financial help from family to move into a new apartment. You may need a recommendation from a friend to find a new job. The neighbor who offers to watch your child while you go to court is an angel.

When getting help from friends, put them in a rotation so that you do not depend on any one friend too much. A friend may be willing to watch your child every once in a while, but if it turns into a constant request, you'll soon find your friends less willing to help. This is the same for friends you call for moral support. A phone call here and there is okay, but if you're calling your friend nearly every day, you'll soon find your relationship strained. Although most friends are willing to help, this help only extends so far.

One of our friends moved back in with her mother after separating from her husband. Her husband wasn't willing to pay spousal or child support, and she was going to find herself on the streets since she had just had a baby and was on unpaid maternity leave. Her mother was more than happy to help, and also to have time to spend with her new grandson!

There are times your family won't be able to help. Some of your family members are already in their own relationships with their own children. They have problems of their own and might not be able to bear the burden of your difficulties at the moment. However, if they volunteer to take the kids for the night so you can sleep in, you should accept gratefully and return the favor graciously.

Family and friends can be the most valuable resource to help you through your divorce. They will be the most understanding about the challenges you have to face. Accept their help with grace.

Note from Leah...

Divorce sucks! I couldn't imagine going through it alone. I am fortunate that I have many fabulous friends and family members who helped me through this. I also have friends in similar situations, and we've learned to help each other out. If a friend needs a sitter to go on a date, I watch the kids, and vice-versa. Start bartering. Rely on friends and family.

Note from Robin...

During my divorce, I found out a lot about my friends and family. Mainly, I found my family less supportive than my friends. My friends, on the other hand, saw more of the actions of my ex than my family was allowed to see. They were emotionally supportive, sympathetic, and helpful in ways I couldn't imagine. Divorce raised the importance of friendship to me, to the point that I consider many of my friends a part of my family.

Activity: Reach out to that friend or family member who offered to help and take them up on their offer.

Enhance Basic Skills

Now is when you learn what your ex's strengths were. These are some of the challenges you may have to face. You may already be proficient with computers, but your ex may have been the one who did all the troubleshooting at home. You may know how to cook spaghetti, but other than that you are clueless in the kitchen. Take the time to research and learn how to do those things on your own.

The internet is down! Call man to fix it! Really?! That needs to stop. You can learn to hook up the internet, configure a router, and replace a modem. No secret testosterone magic makes that happen. There is customer service and your own determination to get it done. When you finally get it working, you will be so surprised at how easy it is to do. Guys make it seem like a herculean task when they fix a computer problem. If you think girls can't get computers, look up Grace Hopper.

Cooking is not a secret recipe your mother never shared with you. Most professional chefs are men. You don't have to learn cooking from your mom. In fact, some of you may have mothers who don't know how to cook! The internet is a great place to learn about cooking. There are articles on the most basic skills, such as how to fry an egg and how to bake a potato. Start with those, and you will soon find yourself making homemade gnocchi in a less than a year. Also, braiding a ponytail is not a mysterious wonder of modern technology. There are videos online showing how to do little girls' hair.

Learning basic home repair is a must. You may have to buy a few tools here and there, but you can save a ton in the long run. There will come a time or two when you'll need to bring in a repair person. When they do the repair, watch carefully. You can learn a lot. Fixing a running toilet can turn into an empowering moment when you realize how easy it is.

A woman we knew took a class to help her learn the basic skills she needed. She learned how to have a basic repair kit, exchanged tips with other women, and gained the confidence to try to fix some basic things around the house. The class was inexpensive and also offered lessons for men to help them learn the things their wives knew during the marriage.

Continue to enhance your basic skills to help you face the new challenges you face. You'll find excellent resources to help you learn how to do many things yourself that you had previously depended on your spouse to do.

Note from Leah...

When first separating from my ex, my 75-year-old grandmother told me not to worry and that I would be amazed at how much I could do on my own. She was right! I have learned how to handle so much on my own. My ex always managed all the computer issues in the household. I had to educate myself on all the various synched devices and backup storage. It is freeing to be able to handle the things you once relied on another person for. Don't doubt yourself, do your research, you can do much more than you realize.

Note from Robin...

The remote control and I have issues. I hate it when I can't get the fucking thing to work. Eventually, I got the secret. Fiddle with the thing until something happens.

After all, guys do that with the female body, and they seem to get it eventually. That's the same technique they've been using for the TV remote. Try it. You *will* get it to work.

Activity: Check the internet for your next "How-to" project. You just may be amazed at how easy it is to do yourself.

Chapter Four

MOVING FORWARD

When you're ready, it will be time to move forward. Divorce is not just about two people separating. It's about restructuring your entire life, including your social life and the people in it. You have friends from childhood, friends from work, and friends from marriage. These friendships grow into intricate social circles creating a web of support.

Moving forward will also involve dating again when you're ready. We will discuss the variety of ways people approach dating after divorce along with some pieces of valuable advice. This chapter is a blueprint for setting up your new social life and preserving what remains of your old one. We will also discuss how reevaluating your career and living well will help move your life forward.

Social Life-ing

Dates with Friends ~ "Couples" v. "Singles" ~ Social Groups ~ Social Media

Social Life-ing is a term used to describe life outside of work and family. It encompasses outings with friends, online engagements, and participation in social groups. Some people are naturals at establishing a social life. They can be dropped in the middle of any city and become part of a social circle within a very short period. Some of these people have learned how to do this as a result of living in several different places throughout their lives.

Whether you're an expert level social-lifer or new to the entire experience of restructuring a social life, there are ways to get there faster and easier. The sooner your social life is established, the sooner you will be able to move forward with other parts of your life.

Dates with Friends

Even if you made off with the house, the kids, the IRA, the stocks, and the friends, your social life will need to be restructured, because the one thing you no longer have is the spouse. Often, the less resentful partner makes off with the friends and sometimes the in-laws as well. But there are times a quiet partner loses social footing for the simple reason that they don't do enough to engage with their established social contacts. Take the initiative to move forward in your life and start with your friends.

Social life-ing isn't only for the weekends. A quick coffee date or lunch with friends is a great way to catch up and relax. While married, breaks in the day might have been a time to run errands or power through a few things at work. But this time is valuable and should be spent on your social life for many reasons.

First, having dates with friends will keep you from isolating yourself. Do NOT take your self-pity and depression with you on the date. After the divorce, it's easy to wallow in pity and depression. Meeting with friends gets you out of a rut and into a safe social scene, especially if you're not ready to date. This is helpful when starting a new social life.

Second, you will learn things from your friends that you never did before. A short date allows for sharing between two people that would otherwise be lost at a party or other group gathering. After a series of meetings with the same person, you may find a theme will emerge. You and a particular friend may always talk about art, and another friend will always be the one you share stories about work with, and yet another will share about relationships. Keep the conversation on them. They have been there for you through your divorce, it's time to listen and not complain.

Finally, the emotional support you gain from dates with your friends is priceless. A little burst of friendship and a sympathetic ear in the middle of the day is enough to give you a lift that carries you through the rest of your day. Don't hog the conversation by talking about your ex. It's time to talk about your future, not your past.

Take a break in the middle of the day to have a date with friends. A short coffee break or lunch will help you feel more centered and well rested. Use your times with friends as a little platform to move forward with your social life.

Note from Leah...

When first separated, I was advised by a good friend "to go out every chance you get." She then explained how it is very easy to fall into a rut due to depression, and hole up in your home. I have her in the back of my mind whenever I get invited to an event. I am creating a new life, and part of that is doing things outside of my comfort zone. I have had such fun new experiences and met many new good friends as a result.

Note from Robin...

I meet with friends at least twice a week to "catch up." It's easy to say that there's no time for it after divorce because of work, the kids, and the ongoing battles with the ex. There are days I feel like I have to force myself to do it. But once the date is set, I feel obligated to go. I'm grateful afterward. We usually meet for coffee at an in between location. Some friends I meet with regularly every week, others I meet once every couple of months. It's a special time to bond in the middle of the day.

Activity: Make a date with a friend. You'll come home feeling so much better. Laughter is key.

"Couples" v. "Singles."

Part of moving forward in your social life is maintaining the friendships you already have. You have friends that are both "*Single*" (not in a relationship) and "*Couples*" (in a relationship, married or not). You will need both types of friendships and both will have much to offer.

If you've been in a relationship for any length of time, chances are you've become friends with your partner's friends. Double dates, birthday parties, and work functions have only strengthened those relationships. After the divorce, the friends often get divided up like property. As much as people say they would like to remain friends with both of you, this is rarely the case. There is usually one reluctant participant in divorce. During the process, the scissors of animosity and accusations will cut through the intricate web of your social life. Friends will take sides. It happens.

One of our friends, recently divorced, came up with a great idea to socialize with both his couple and single friends. He arranged a getaway vacation and invited his single friends for the first half and the couple friends for the second half.

Don't be intimidated by couples. Although your married life may have involved a social schedule full of couple activities, you don't have to feel left out because you're now divorced. Keep in contact with those friends! Some may feel awkward because you are now divorced so make the first move and give them a call every once and a while. They will come to realize that friendships can survive a divorce.

When you were married, did you lose contact with friends that are single? Now is the time to broaden your social circle and re-establish contact with those friends. Your calendar is going to open up with a variety of new happenings that you never had time for before. Your ex may not have been into certain activities which you avoided while you were married. This is no longer an issue. Reconnect with those single friends and let them introduce you to new experiences!

Note from Leah...

During my marriage, I managed to have a handful of single friends. There were some new friends and some from before marriage. I quickly realized after I married that it was crucial to remain in contact with my single friends. They are the ones who can go on last minute trips out of town, shopping, or join you for that last minute happy hour. I maintained these friendships throughout my marriage and made many more once divorced. It is important to keep these friendships alive when you are single.

If you haven't already done so, now is the time to rekindle these friendships or be open to new ones. I was fortunate to be introduced to a single woman friend at work. We were chatting and realized that we live right near one another. We have become fast friends, and she's a huge part of my life now. Similarly, at a school bowling event, I was paired with a mom, and we realized we live in the same complex. She is also divorced with children. These two women have now become such a significant part of my life. We hang out all the time. Be open to meeting new people. You never know when you're going to find a new best friend or TWO to add to your group!

Note from Robin...

I've had a more difficult time maintaining friendships with couples I knew during marriage. Most of the time, I've been reaching out to one-half of the couple and keeping the friendship alive on that end. We meet for coffee or lunch and continue to keep in contact that way.

I've met a lot of other people who are in limbo with their relationships. They are just separated, are newly divorced, or in a troubled marriage. I've found that these are the easiest relationships for me to form right now because we have so much in common. These are wonderful people to become friends with. We are in the same place and understand how complicated a difficult divorce can be. These friends don't judge and need to establish a new social circle as much as I do.

Activity: Schedule a dinner with a mix of your couple and single friends.

Social Groups

A social group is a group of people brought together by a single interest. Social groups are established by a third party and meet officially but in a casual setting. They are easy to join, often free, and an excellent way to meet new people.

Social groups are not a new concept although the variety of social groups has grown. In the past, social groups were most commonly local charity groups, fan clubs, sports leagues, or game organizations. These days, those groups still exist but in a different way. A sports league, for example, can be a social group that you can join for a short period. Many offer co-ed experiences with teams for flag football, softball, kickball, bowling, golf, archery, badminton and more. Many of the participants are also looking to meet new people. There's a nominal fee for joining, you meet great people, and bond with them through a shared experience.

We had a friend who joined a group for swing dancing. He couldn't dance to save his life, but wanted to try something new after getting out of a nine-year marriage. He didn't have any high expectations about becoming a professional dancer and had never taken a class before. He wasn't the type to go to clubs but thought this would be a good skill to have when he started dating in the future. He's met a great circle of friends and now takes his dates to the social group now and then.

Even if you're not an active sort, there are groups for you too. There are book clubs, gardening clubs, movie reviewers, music groups, board game meet-ups, and art clubs. There are even groups that meet for the sole purpose of discussing types of computer programming languages. Social groups offer an excellent way to meet like-minded people without feeling the pressure of hosting or being obligated to attend an event.

You might feel uncomfortable moving forward into a new social circle, especially if you depended on your ex to pave the way for you. Your self-confidence will increase when you create your own group of friends with interests that are similar to yours. Being independent in your social life will help you to grow into who you truly are as an individual.

Note from Leah...

There are so many different groups out there in this day and age. I have friends that met new people through running groups, adult soccer, PTA, and stroller exercising for parents with young kids. The list goes on and on. In the past, I have orchestrated a new recipe exchange idea. A group of friends gets together once a month and whoever hosts cooks dinner. Everyone makes copies of their recipes to share. It's a great way to stay in touch with your friends, and simultaneously learn new healthy dinner recipes to add to your portfolio of meals. I also share a love for essential oils. I have met so many like-minded individuals who also share this love. If you're having troubles finding where to start, think about what you love. Then, look up a group or start your own.

Note from Robin...

I'm more of the type to join a book club and I'm terrible at sports, but at my brother's insistence I joined a flag football team. Some of the people who participated were couples and some were singles. I met many new people and learned a lot about football. In between games, we would chat about strategy. After games, we would celebrate our win or comfort each other on our loss at a local bar or restaurant. I now know a lot more about the game, and I'm able to understand and enjoy watching sports too.

Activity: Look up social groups in your area with your top three areas of interests. Sign up for one.

Social Media

Social media is a big part of our world. Most people engage in it some way or other. Social media platforms usually involve creating a page or board. There are options for communicating with people privately in addition to having your public profile.

Create a new page or image for your life post-divorce and don't friend the ex. He or she does not need to be stalking you through social media. You should be choosy about who you allow to follow or friend, and watch what you post. Remember, even if your account is private, posting things that can be used against you is not worth the risk.

Social media can be a great way to meet new people as long as you take precautions. Relationships can grow online. You are newly single. It's not about finding the next great love of your life because you're still dealing with the recent separation from the *last* supposed love of your life.

Reach out to the online world, but be careful as you do. Try something new and different. The conversations you have can broaden your social base and help you move forward towards creating friendships in the real world.

If you're still cautious about being online, there are other outlets that allow you more privacy. There are sites with no individual pages or boards. These can be in the form of current event feeds or other sites with online commentary. If you prefer to remain anonymous while venturing into conversations online, this is an excellent way to go. You can establish an online name unrelated to your own. The sites are always open, and you never have to feel obligated to respond.

Note from Leah...

There is always a new 'hot' social site to be part of. There are sites to stay connected internationally, ones that allow you to advertise your day through videos, and several dating sites. It is a way to feel connected when you may not have the time to contact a friend or family in person. I have different avenues of social media that I use to stay connected to family and friends. It helps me feel connected by giving me a glimpse into their lives.

There are also various dating and friend sites. I have met many new people through these sites as well. I have continued to be open-minded to the people that come into my life, whether a new friend or a cute guy. I truly believe every person comes into your life for a reason. You may make an unexpected connection when you are not looking. You may be inspired by someone to start a new career or business. You never know what is in store for you. Who knows? Maybe you'll meet that hot Chippendale and fulfill your Magic Mike fantasy.

Note from Robin…

Being social is a lot of work. I don't always have a few hours to spend on parties or events. Going online and connecting with people satisfies the itch to engage with others and keeps me from dwelling on work.

I've known people who moved to a new city and used online engagements to establish their social circles *before* they moved. They find the active forums where they live and join in conversations. Within a short time, they're invited to events where they get to meet others in real life. They follow up the event with more online engagement and soon they have established a base of casual friends to hang out with.

Activity: Try a new social site for dating or to find new friends. Log in and explore.

Dating

Online ~ Real World ~ Dating Privacy ~ Re-Runs ~ New Experiences

Yes. We are talking about this. Ready or not, dating is in your future. You have been burned or participated in a little burning yourself in your last relationship. Now, it is time to let the ashes seep into the ground, let the rain come, and allow new flowers to bloom.

Some of you may be ready to take the plunge immediately, but there are those of you who are out of practice and fearful of venturing back into the dating world. Take heart. If you haven't dated for a while, there's a way to break into it without being traumatized.

Online Dating

Depending on how long you were married and out of the dating scene, you will quickly realize that a majority of the dating happening in today's world is through online dating sites. Online dating doesn't have the stigma it used to have. You can choose from a variety of sites that can connect you to people of similar backgrounds, interests, religious beliefs and lifestyle habits. It's convenient and can travel with you on your phone.

Someone we knew tried this and went to a site catering to people like her, spiritual and socially active. She was extremely embarrassed to confess she tried online dating but soon found she could connect with others like her. Fresh after a separation, she wasn't ready for anything very serious and the online dating gave her a start after being married for almost eight years.

Before you begin dating online, here are some important tips to remember. Number One: Do not use your actual name in your username. It's best to keep that anonymous as a matter of safety because there can be questionable people online. Have fun creating a username, because you will be stuck with it after that depending on the site you're on. You're old enough to know that creating a username can give a first impression. Anything with sexual overtones will send just that message – sex. If you're serious about dating, and not just hooking up, create a username that's memorable, not sexual. "titsnass69" or "2big4U", although memorable, are usernames that send the message that you want sex, not a date.

Number Two: Set up a separate email account for the sole purpose of online dating. The last thing you want is to be bombarded with spam and emails from strange people, and this will also give you a way to delete an online dating profile along with that email for a fresh start.

Number Three: Be tolerant. You will hear both good and bad in regards to online dating. There will be interesting and intelligent people you meet online, as well as strange people. The same can be said for actual dating.

Online dating looks like it's here to stay in some form or another. Try it out, stay safe, and enjoy it! You never know what might happen!

Note from Leah...

There are never enough hours in a day. I quickly realized this once I moved into my new place. With fifty percent custody and a full-time job, I didn't have much time to meet people. With a push from a friend and a glass of wine in hand, I created an online profile on a popular dating site. I've been very fortunate to meet some cool people. However, many people are looking to hook up, and they won't be shy about it.

Some people are just looking to hook-up and, yes, maybe you are too! But don't let them know that. There are many dating sites - some are good, some are bad. They all have different reputations. It's easy to spot the people who just want to hook up. Some are blatantly honest about it with user names like letsbangheadboards. One favorite was skilledtongueforyou (come on, really!? haha). Some are honest about the casual hookup and others will make it clear that they are looking for something more serious. So explore and have fun with it.

With this advice in mind, I became open to socializing with all types of people. Some of the most fun men I met have been younger than I am. To get my feet wet, I eased into online dating sites with some coffee dates. It was a great learning experience. I continued to go on dates and was open minded to food and restaurants. Those ended up being some of my best dates!

You're newly single, and while you're redefining yourself, it's ok to just date and enjoy. When I first went on the dating sites, I had an idea of what kind of guy I wanted to meet, the type of guy that I felt would work well in my new life. As time went on I met a guy, and another, and several more. My view of what I *thought* I wanted began to change. What you think you need in your life at one point can be entirely different six months later. Just enjoy meeting new people. If you meet someone you can have pure good old fashion fun with, go with it. Enjoy being free, and enjoy the great sex. Have some fun with your new life. Remember, YOU are creating YOUR story. Make it a good one!

Note from Robin...

On my first date after divorce, I had a really good time. My date picked out the activity, he paid for it and led the way. I had been used to planning activities when I was married. It was nice to have someone else take charge!

Activity: Practice writing your dating profile page.

Real World Dating

Real World Dating is an entirely different animal. It's an easy way to get to know a person socially. No promises are made. You may have met someone online or through friends and are about to take it to the next level. Real World Dating can be nerve racking. Remember that chapter on disappointment? Real World Dating is where it's time to have realistic expectations about the date and what it means.

A Real World Date doesn't mean you're getting married or jumping into the sack with the person. Right after a divorce isn't the time to fall in love. You have been there and done that. Real World Dating is a way to vet a person to see if you can get along and to see if there are any defects in that person's character that are unacceptable to you.

When you set up your Real World Date, meet separately in a public place. The times where the guy picks up the girl at her home is archaic and awkward. Dating is much more casual now. Even dinner seems like too much for the first date. Usually, the first date will be meeting for coffee or wine, or sometimes with a group of friends. Bringing someone to a group of casual friends serves a greater purpose. You can see how this person interacts with others who are like you. Are they socially challenged? Too opinionated? Now is the time to find out. Take your time and keep it casual. If there's any connection, you can proceed to dinner or something more formal and intimate.

You've been around the block a few times. You're an adult, and you know many people. Even though you're going through one of the most difficult times in your life emotionally, it's more important than ever to trust your intuition when it comes to Real World Dating. The most important word in the phrase "trust your intuition" is not the word *intuition*, it's the word *trust.* This means that you will have to put trust in yourself, even when others say you're wrong. Your ex may be telling you that you're a bad parent. Trust your intuition. You are offended because you are a good parent. Your kids may be saying that they hate you. Trust your intuition. It hurts because it is untrue. Your blind date may remind you of your ex. Trust your intuition. Run away.

A Real World Date also doesn't mean you need to see that person again. If you think that the date is not going well, leave. It's ok to leave right at that moment if you feel strongly about it. Your intuition is the inner you, giving you guidance. That's why they say, "What does your gut tell you?" Although you may not be able to articulate what might feel wrong, your brain remembers and sends a series of signals out as a warning. You will get goose bumps, chills, or feel suddenly nervous and apprehensive. Your gut is saying, "Hey there, you! Something is wrong here!" Take the time to step back and analyze the situation. You don't have to react immediately, but don't discount what your gut is telling you. Trust your intuition because the truth is inside you.

If there's no chemistry or something throws you off, there's no reason to keep seeing that person. If you're not ready for a relationship and just interested in getting to know someone of the opposite sex, Real World Dating is a way to explore your options.

Note from Leah...

It's scary going on a first date with a person because all the various emotions kick in. *"Am I going to like him? I hope he's as cute in person. Oh shit, what if I am not attracted to him?"...* That is what goes through my head anyhow. But as I've been continually going on first dates, it has gotten easier and become a lot of fun.

I enjoy meeting new people, and I'm quite social, so it's fun to talk with people and hear about the various adventures in their lives. Plus, you never know when you may make a connection, so you have to be willing to put yourself out there. Just use your intuition. For example, I went on a date with a guy, and I was noticing several red flags, including the fact that he has not been in a relationship longer than three months...ever!! For a guy in his mid 30's, that is a problem. So proceed with caution but have fun! You can typically pick up on a lot of someone's character by chatting with them beforehand. So go with your gut. Get out there, and have some fun dating!

Note from Robin...

There were times when I thought about various ex's, "Is he really stupid? Or is he really out to get me?" I always gave an ex the benefit of the doubt and didn't listen to my intuition. After a while, I tuned in. You may be thinking logically. You may be a reasonable person. But divorce has a way of making people both illogical and unreasonable. If you still have a good head on your shoulders, remember that might not be true of your ex. Trust your intuition, in Real World Dating, and in the divorce itself.

Activity: Write about your dream date. Be detailed. What's the weather like, atmosphere? What music is playing? Have fun with it!

<u>Dating Privacy</u>

There is no need for your ex to know if you are dating. It will only cause trouble. Until you are exclusive with one person, there is no reason to divulge any information. The less said, the better. Whether you left your ex, or the other way around, it doesn't matter. Once your ex finds out that you're dating, it can escalate the conflict in your divorce and make moving forward difficult.

Nothing can piss off an ex more than knowing that you're dating. How dare you? You should be mourning his or her loss, not having parties and dates with friends. Keep any new relationships on the "DL." Flaunting a new relationship in front of an ex will only make things worse.

If you have kids, don't let them know. You've just gotten divorced. There's no need to rush into anything. You don't have to invite any new dates to Thanksgiving or Christmas. Until you are in an exclusive, long-term, serious relationship with a person, it's best to keep your dating life separate from your kids. Having your kids meet multiple people that you're dating is not only troubling to the kids but sends a terrible message to everyone: you are unstable. Dating around is fine. Introducing your kids to everyone you're dating is not.

At some point, you might become serious about someone. The big question here is whether or not you tell the ex. That's a tough one. The noble thing to do is to say,

"Ex, I wanted to let you know that I've met someone and it's become serious." But how noble are we?

Often, relationships just *evolve* into something exclusive and long-term. It's not like we are dating someone casually and then, POOF, we are in a serious relationship. Often, the ex discovers you're serious about someone before you might even be aware of it yourself. After all, even before you become serious about someone, you may introduce them to a couple of friends. Those friends may know your ex or know some people who do. Remember? People like to talk.

It's best to keep your dating life private for as long as you can. Take your time getting to know a person before you start introducing them to your friends. There is no rush, and if the person you're dating cares about you, they will be patient about being introduced to your friends and family.

Note from Leah...

It is crucial to keep it quiet. This advice has come my way on numerous occasions from different single friends. If kids are involved, it is hard for them to get attached to a new person in their lives, and then all of a sudden that person isn't around anymore, and they don't understand why. That reason alone is good enough to keep it quiet until it's serious.

It will likely be that you will run into your ex on some of the online dating sites. Every social site is different, but all have the same "block" function. Find it and block yourself quickly. Note that some of the sites show every time a person has viewed you or looked at your page. You don't need your ex monitoring your usage. Just block! Learn how to do this. Keep your dating life private from your ex.

One of my good friends had a great story about dating online:

"The day I finally got the nerve to try out a dating site, I went through all the motions of filling out the profile, and then boom – my profile was live. I'm thinking, "Wow, this is fun! It's a man shopping site, sweet!" Within 15 minutes of this, my buzz was killed when I saw an oddly familiar username. I look at the photo, and sure enough, there was an ex. I'll tell you, his profile was not new, which made me realize he had been on it for a while already. Anyhow, I quickly blocked myself from his view and any of my searches. It's probably best to not be on the same site as your ex. It's just kind of awkward."

Note from Robin...

It's so important to keep a new relationship on the DL after divorce, especially if you were the one who asked for the divorce. The last thing you want is for your ex to think you had an affair while you were married.

After separating, I kept a new relationship on the DL for months. After the new relationship was out in the open, it changed the divorce from friendly to ferocious very quickly. If they care about you, whoever you're dating will understand that you need to keep things quiet. If it's a casual relationship, there's no reason to flaunt it on social media. You and your ex have many friends in common, and word will quickly spread. It's easier to get through your divorce without the added pressure of defending yourself.

Activity: Review your dating activities and ensure that your online profiles are private.

Re-Runs

A Re-Run is a person you've dated before who you are trying to date again. The first time around, this person didn't work out. Time has passed, and you may be wondering why. Then, once you start up the relationship again you remember: the person was petty, jealous, lazy, or rude. By then, it's too late. You're back into an old relationship that you had worked hard to get out of so many years before.

Re-Runs are a bad idea for several other reasons. First, you may go back to an ex because you're lonely. You've become used to having someone share your life, and now that person is gone. It's far too easy to ring up an ex after a breakup, and just as difficult to get rid of them the second time around. Remember, being lonely is better than being in a bad relationship. You are moving forward in your life – not backward. Meet new people. Don't regurgitate old, dysfunctional relationships.

Do not think that you can just ring up an ex to see what that person is up to. Any attraction you had before may come flooding back, clouding your judgment. If you broke up because the relationship was inequitable, there was cheating, or the person didn't like your personality or intelligence, not much will have changed over time.

Note from Leah...

Before marriage, I was notorious for calling up the ex-boyfriend. It happens, and it is common. However, now that you have been married and divorced it is time to keep moving forward. I can tell you that going back to the ex in my twenties did not serve me well and created lots of drama. This time around I take an entirely different approach.

I took Robin's advice with the 'No Re-Runs.' It's served me well so far, and as a result, I have met a lot of really cool men. Stay open-minded and take your time with dating. You are recreating yourself and need to heal. When the time is right, he or she will be there waiting. Enjoy this time.

Note from Robin...

In my late teens and early twenties, I loved Re-Runs. I found myself constantly going back to old boyfriends instead of looking for new ones. It was a constant merry-go-round of the same horses, same direction, and same disappointing result. At some point, I put a stop to the Re-Runs and ventured out. I ended up married to someone I had never dated before and stayed married for nearly 18 years.

Activity: Make a list of exes and put them on a Do Not Call List.

<u>New Experiences</u>

Open yourself up to new experiences, sexually speaking and otherwise. If you find yourself going through your grocery list mentally while having sex, it's probably time to spice things up. You're not a virgin anymore. No need to act coy. Own your sexuality and experiment.

If you're not ready to share your body with anyone yet, remember: Nobody will know your body, like YOU know your body. Your ex knew your body and the sex might have been great (or maybe not), so don't hesitate to make a little love with yourself. Light some candles, put on some music, take a hot bubble bath and get personal with yourself. If you're going to attract the person who is going to enhance and compliment the person you already are, then you need to be that person first. Practice self-love! Afterward, don't feel any shame. You are loving yourself!!

If you're a woman, don't be shy. Buy a vibrator if you haven't already. In fact, buy more than one. Make sure it's rechargeable because you might end up spending a small fortune on batteries. There are plenty available online, complete with reviews from previous customers. However, don't do your research at a coffee shop. Those sites are often blocked. We tried.

We know a guy who tried speed dating for a new dating experience. Even though he didn't like it, it turned out that a lot of other people during the event didn't either. He ended up having drinks with a bunch of them afterward to complain about it. Even though the experience was not a good one, he gained from the new experience by making new friends at the event.

Enjoy meeting new people and learning about different men and women of various ages. Just have fun with it, and don't take it too seriously. It's not the time to find a relationship yet, so make as many new friends as you can. You never know what opportunities will come from it. Life is too short not to have fun! And kissing is fun no matter what age!

Keep your emotions in check and keep it casual!

Note from Leah...

I have met so many men of all ages with similar interests to mine. It's been awesome meeting so many like-minded men. It's fun! I never really did this in my younger single years and, looking back, I have no idea why I didn't! This time around I'm going with it. Enjoy the moment and if that moment happens to consist of a hot man (or woman!) – kiss them!

I have several friends living vicariously through my dating life. It's been quite entertaining to the say the least.

DO buy a vibrator for a newly single friend.

Note from Robin...

New experiences don't have to start or end in the bedroom. See a psychic and have your cards read. Ask about your love life. I recently got my cards read at the county fair. It was a fun, first-time experience and one off the bucket list.

Activity: What's on your bucket list? Travel? Languages? Threesomes? Not only should you make a bucket list, but you should also start checking items off of it as soon as possible.

Career

Find Your Passion ~ Re-evaluate Your Career ~ Start a Business

Moving forward will include a potential change in your career. Now that you've split from your partner, the income contributed by that partner is gone. There may be new expenses like child support and alimony. If you think that because you're a woman you avoid paying alimony, think again. We know several high-earning professional women who have had to pay child support and alimony to their former spouses. If your role in marriage was the one of stay-at-home mom or dad, it's time to start bringing in the bacon.

Find Your Passion

You are in a new chapter of your life. In this period of change, you may realize the passion you always had and didn't act on. Something new that you just love might call to you now. If that is the case, what better time than to start something new whether it's a business idea, a new way of eating or exercising, or that craft you were always so good at making.

Finding your passion means discovering what you want to do with your life. You are now at a time of personal growth, revisiting your past goals and seeing if they still apply to your life now. You may have had dreams that you put aside once you married. Do these have a place in your life now? Is this something you can pursue?

Your passion may be something new. You won't know until you venture into new activities. Finding your passion is a process. It takes time. When you find your passion, motivation will come effortless, work will be easier, and your outlook will be more positive.

Being passionate about something will help you find confidence and happiness. The effort you put forth in finding your passion can be fun and ultimately fulfilling. Be creative and explore. If you have an interest in something like painting, try a class. If you have an interest in cooking, join a group. It's *these* interests and talents that lead you to your passion. So before you go any further, find that passion and do what you love! We dare you to make a list of what your perfect day would look like, and start making the things on that list part of your life.

Note from Leah...

Your passion may not be something that is known to you. That is okay. There are many resources out there to help you to discover your passion. Do some research and see what resonates with you. You may be surprised by what sparks your interest.

I have several passions. I love to help people. That's why I'm writing this book! My other passion is inspiring people to live a healthy lifestyle. Life is short, and you only have one shot at it, so it's important to treat yourself well. As a result of this mindset, you will be happier and have more energy. Why wouldn't you want to practice healthy habits? Start small and one day at a time, and you will be surprised at how quickly your body responds to you treating it well.

Note from Robin...

When I first married, I was a terrible cook. Eventually, I learned, but I was limited to what my husband and children wanted to eat. After I had divorced, I explored cooking in a new way and found a passion for creating gourmet meals. I enjoy hunting down fresh ingredients and trying new foods. I enjoy cooking for friends. It's a passion that makes me happy!

Activity: Make a list of your perfect day. Incorporate at least one thing each day. You may find your passion as a result.

Re-evaluate Your Career

Your married life meant that your career choices, in part, were made with your relationship in mind. Maybe you didn't take a job, because it was in a different state, or didn't take a promotion because there wouldn't have been time for your relationship. Possibly, you picked a career that catered to your spouse's hours, or that gave you the flexibility to stay at home with the kids.

We cannot live our lives with someone else without our lives being changed, for better or for worse. We make sacrifices, concessions, and negotiate duties. After a divorce, although there are still some considerations when children are involved, your career can now be all about YOU.

Re-evaluating your career is a huge part of moving forward. It takes time, thought, and careful planning to make a successful career change. The enjoyable part of re-evaluating your career and possibly making a change is that it creates a positive mental space for you. Your days will be less focused on the divorce and more on your future.

Your career is important. It is no longer secondary to someone else's wants or needs. Re-evaluating whether or not you are engaged in a job you want can help you find more satisfaction in your life. Move forward. Move up. Leave that dead-end job you've been stuck in. Write that book. Go back to school.

Note from Leah...

It is time to re-evaluate yourself and your life. What do *you* want? What is the career that *you* always dreamed about? This world is full of abundance and opportunity. It is time to achieve your dream life.

While married, I went back to school to earn my MBA. When I look back at how I pulled off going back to school, working full-time with two young boys, and being married, it makes me quite proud and a bit amazed. I am not sure how I pulled it off, but I did... and as a result, I'm a better person.

You can find the time to do it! You just have to have the willingness and desire. During this period I would hear people say "*but I don't have enough time*" but that's just an excuse. If you want it badly enough, you *make* time! If I can do it, so can you.

Note from Robin...

I love my work. I love being productive and involved. Being able to say that I've contributed to something helps my self-confidence. I've always recommended that some women try a career in hair, skin, or massage. If you've ever paid for good cut and color, you know that this can be a well-paying job. Added to that are the flexible hours. If you have children, the appointments can be when the kids are in school. My own skin care lady has an area in her home, complete with all the professional gear. Her 3-year old acts as "front desk secretary." Her client list has grown to the point where she's two weeks out on appointments and her husband has offered to build an addition to the house for her business.

I decided to re-evaluate my career during my marriage rather than after divorce. I went back to school and made MY career MY priority. It was the most selfish thing I ever did during my marriage, and it felt GREAT!

Through the process of going back to school, I found that the career I already had made me very happy, however, the skills I learned in school helped with what I was doing before. It's never too late to have the career you always wanted. I was the not the oldest student in my class when I returned to school. I made new friends and loved expanding my mind. The career you desire is obtainable. You can do it.

Activity: What did you want to do when you grew up? Is that what you're doing now? What do you want to be doing now? Answer these questions.

<u>Start your own business</u>

For some, getting divorced opens up possibilities in other areas of life. Some people go back to school, some go back to work, and some pursue their dreams. We've noticed an interesting trend with friends who have gotten divorced. Even though most are working regular jobs, many have started new businesses. It's as if passion blooms when they become single, and they move forward in their lives by starting the business they've always wanted to have.

There *are* a few warnings when starting a business. Some businesses are complete money pits and can drain you. If you are starting a business, it's vital to have a solid plan and make lots of contingency plans, too. Plan for the unexpected.

If your business is purely service based, it's less likely that you'll be put in a precarious financial predicament, especially if the service you're providing is only provided by you. If your business involves a product, it may be a while before you see a profit. Many business owners we have known have been on the verge of bankruptcy more than once. It takes strength and persistence to succeed as a business owner.

You can make money doing practically anything. Some jobs don't necessarily involve putting in a lot of money and time towards a fancy degree. If you love animals, there's pet sitting and grooming. If you love children, there's in-home daycare, tutoring, and teaching. If you have a particular talent or interest in anything, there is a job out there for you.

We know a woman who loved chocolate and partnered up with some friends and started a little chocolate making store. After a year of ups and downs, they attracted the interest of an investor. Now, they have a 15,000 square foot building and a thriving business. Another woman we know loved organic skin products. She worked out of her garage for several years. Her products now sell in nearly every organic grocery store in the U.S. Her products are expensive and in demand. It goes to show that even loving your skin can be translated into a career.

It makes no sense getting a job in accounting if you hate balancing your own budget. It also doesn't make sense to be chained to a desk in a nine-to-five job when you'd rather be outside. There are plenty of jobs that can take you out into the fresh air. We've spent a lot of time in this book, challenging you to try new things, and explore hidden interests and talents you never knew existed.

Even with all the pitfalls involved in starting a business, there are definite benefits that can make it all worthwhile. The first is the prospect of becoming your own boss. You can control your workflow and your hours. For those who are now single with children, this is an opportunity to work at home with the kids. If it's a brick and mortar business, you can also bring the children with you. You also guarantee your employment. No one is going to lay you off. There are tax advantages available and grants, especially if you are a woman, a minority, or both. Along with that is the pride in creating something worthwhile, providing a service or product that is needed, and giving back to the world.

Note from Leah...

When I was young and in college working a waitressing job, I remember thinking to myself, as I was lying out on the beach in the early afternoon before work, "I'm never going to do well in a 40-hour workweek job." Fast forward a decade, and there I was, working in corporate world many hours a week and not happy. I earned my MBA and realized quickly that a change was needed. I am creating a new life that is all my own. I'm no longer married but need to make sure my children are taken care of and that I can provide the best life for them possible. Now is the time to embark on a new adventure.

Note from Robin...

I have always been a business owner. Other business owners I know say that once you own your own business, you are ruined and unable to work for anyone else again. The other thing that business owners say is that they work harder for themselves than they ever did for other people. This is absolutely true. Business owners will work late and make many personal sacrifices.

Activity: Write down a business you might like to start. Make detailed plans.

Living Well

Food ~ Wine ~ Travel

When moving forward in your life, it's important to put effort into living well. Living well doesn't have to be expensive. There's a lot you can accomplish in small areas of your life to help you feel like you're taken care of. During the marriage, you may have put more into living well than your spouse by planning meals or travel. You may have been the recipient of those efforts, and now your spouse is gone. It's important to remember that living well does not just apply to couples. Living well is something everyone should experience.

When the divorce gets rough, living well will remind you that there are pleasures in life. It will give you a healthy perspective on your life by giving you something more than work, chores, and family obligations. This part of the book is to remind you to continue living well, especially after your divorce.

Food

As tempting as it is to go through a drive-thru or eat nothing but spaghetti and ramen, it's important to continue to eat well after the divorce. Eating well doesn't mean eating a lot, and there may have been times during divorce when you did that. Eating well means taking the time to prepare and appreciate the food you put into your body.

We mentioned how you would need to downsize. Downsizing can make meal preparation more challenging. It can be hard to justify making an elaborate meal for yourself when you will eat it in fifteen minutes. Part of the fun in preparing such a meal is sharing it with someone else. This is a perfect time to invite a friend over for dinner and a part of moving forward in your life.

With children, eating well can be a challenge. Kids don't like steaks; they like chicken nuggets. If they're young, children can be messy and challenging eating partners. Often, parents will feed young children separately so they can enjoy their own meal with adults. Some may eat a bit with the children, then have a separate meal later.

As far as eating on your own, fill your kitchen with foods that are healthy for you. Buy fruits and vegetables. You can take the time to fix a lot of food if you can store the remainder for later. For example, you can make a huge pot of chili and then set some aside in the freezer or a few in containers for work. Not only is it more healthy to eat the food you make yourself, but you'll also save money and time by taking the food to work with you.

Eating well is a part of living well and living well is how you move forward in your life. It's more than just grabbing something quick to get through the day. It's a way to nurture yourself and enjoy living.

Note from Leah...

When I first moved to my new home, expenses once shared were now all mine. One way to cut back on expenses is to be aware of the cost of food. I began to cook bigger dishes and freeze half for the following month. I also cut back on take-out.

I found that as a result, I began eating more healthy by packing my own lunch. It also made eating out much more of a treat. The one habit that I was most proud of, and that saved me lots of money, was my daily coffee from the coffee shop. I purchased a latte machine and now make my own fancy coffee. And you know what? I think it is much tastier.

P.S. My healthy eating habits are rubbing off on Robin.

Note from Robin...

Since I've been divorced, I've been more conscious of my eating habits and how I prepare meals. I've noticed that the *quantity* of food I make has decreased, but the *quality* has increased. I use our local farmer's market, where I can buy inexpensive greens. I've grown some of my own vegetables to use every day. Continuing the practice of eating well reminds me that I'm worth it.

Activity: Make a list of your favorite meals. Prepare the top three for the week. Viola! You have your lunch and dinner for the week.

Wine

Part of living well is enjoying good wine. A quote we've heard is, "wine was invented for parents." Well, we know this isn't the case. Wine was created for all. This is why we have dedicated a section to the joys of wine and followed with our personal favorites. Here's our recommendations of health benefits associated with wine during divorce:

1.   Start a monthly wine night with your friends.
2.   If you have more than one kid, you get an extra glass!
3.   It has mental health benefits.
4.   It boosts levels of Omega 3 Fatty acids.
5.   When attending, social events bring your favorite wine. As a result of your kindness, you always have good wine to drink.
6.   It protects against various cancers.
7.   Find out where the local restaurants have a wine night. Grab a friend and go.
8.   It has healthy heart benefits.
9.   If you talk about the ex, you need to do so with wine.
10. It promotes a longer lifespan.

Wine will make you feel better. It can make you feel sexy, horny, happy, funny, sexy, absolutely fabulous, maybe just drunk, and sexy. A word of warning, though: Do NOT drunk dial after enjoying wine.

We joined a wine club started by one of our divorced friends. She invites people over for a "Wine and Dessert Tasting" once a month. Each person brings a bottle of wine and a dessert with the recipe to share. She has over fifty people on her invite list, and at least ten people attend each month. She has even had guests get creative with their recipes. When we visited, we saw a recipe for "Alimony Ambrosia." This particular dessert was even more amusing, given that the chef had waived alimony!

As long as you stick with our suggestions, wine can be a part of living well and moving forward. Just remember, it's W-I-N-E not W-H-I-N-E. Do not talk about the ex, or the divorce, or we will pull your wine card and relegate you to boxed juices.

Note from Leah...

Wine is a necessity for me. I have always enjoyed a nice glass of Pinot Noir, but now, being a newly divorced single parent, it has an entirely new function. I have found a new appreciation for it, and it's a great way to re-connect with friends. It has so many health benefits, and we're not just talking about the antioxidants.

It is perfect for when you just need to relax and take a deep breath from a long day. I enjoy a glass on the days I have had a particularly tough day with my kids, work or the ex. Whatever they may be, it helps to have some good wine on hand for those tough moments. We have included some of our favorites as part of your activity. You're welcome.

Note from Robin...

Wine is best shared. I have some friends who can go through a whole bottle, but I need someone to help me through it! I can rarely do a white wine. I love a dark, husky red wine. Right now, I'm into the Argentinean wines, Malbecs, and Shiraz.

Activity: Find your favorite red or white wines. Check your local Trader Joes, World Market or an online wine club! They are all excellent sources.

Travel

Living well also means creating new memories. What better way than on a road trip? Grab some close friends, jump in the car, and go! The conversations while traveling in a car with good friends is priceless, and it will have you looking back and laughing for months.

The way travel helps you to move forward in your life is by taking you *out* of your present situation. Even though this means physically moving, it has an effect on your mental outlook too. Visiting a new place and seeing new people gives you a wider perspective on your life. Suddenly, the little things that may irritate you at home may not seem so significant. An annoying neighbor is now less annoying than before because you've been able to remove yourself from the situation for a little bit. Problems at work seem less daunting when you've had some time to be away. Even the ex seems less a part of your life when you've had a chance to be somewhere else.

By the time you return home, you are usually eager to do so, and ready to attack any situation. Your house seems different, and you are suddenly inspired to reorganize or clean. You've seen how other people live, or how nice the hotel was, and you now have ideas on creating a better living space. Your mind has had time to regroup and think about things other than work and family, so now you are ready to look at situations in a different way.

We know a gentleman who has been divorced for many years. Always cheerful and positive, he shared his secret with us. "At least once a month," he said, "I get out of town. It doesn't have to be a long trip. Sometimes it's just camping. When I get back, I get so much more work done!"

Traveling with friends is like sugar in your coffee. It sweetens the whole experience. Trips with friends involve more than the actual trip itself. There's all the planning beforehand. Deciding where to go, what to wear, and coordinating departure dates is all part of the bonding experience. After the trip, there is time to share photos with each other and with friends who weren't able to go along. Being divorced doesn't mean that you are required to stay home and be miserable. Experience the world!

Note from Leah...

I love to travel, but one day I woke up and realized I was married, had two kids, worked full time and had no time to travel. This thought saddened me. Now that I'm divorced and recreating my new life I am making sure that traveling is part of it, Vegas with the girls, or Miami. Whatever the city is, I made a pact with myself to be open to the new food and happenings that town has to offer. I try new restaurants that are part of the culture. I truly immerse myself when traveling, and you know what, I don't think about home and all the worries and problems I'm dealing with. It is my time to be 'me' and enjoy getting to know that person. Travel, even if it's only to a cabin in the mountains or a hotel in the city nearby. It counts. Do it. Immerse yourself in the moment, and enjoy the new experiences that come with it.

Note from Robin...

Before I travel, I like to clean my house from top to bottom. This is because by the time I'm done traveling, walking into a clean home makes me feel relaxed and happy. I'm known as a person who continues to work while traveling. I always make sure there's a desk somewhere for me to set up, along with access to a printer and scanner. It may seem like I'm not getting away from work. However, I find that I work on different things when I'm traveling. Since I'm not in the office, other things take priority that I may not have given enough attention to before. Traveling is a great way for me to look at my life differently and approach work from a different direction.

Activity: Make a travel plan. Enjoy the process of putting it together.

Chapter Five

THE LEAP FORWARD

The Leap Forward in your life is about to kick in. You will see your future take shape in relationships, career, and independence. You may be ready to make a move to a new city, start a new romance, or simply celebrate the beginnings of your new life. When you're willing to make the leap, moving forward in your life is an exhilarating experience.

To help you make this leap, we've listed some of the critical areas of your life that will be affected. Change is good, and change with proper planning is even better. We have ways to guide you through these changes and make the leap forward as amazing, thrilling, and fun as it can be.

The Leap to Independence

Bravery ~ Alone is the New Sexy ~ Moving

The first step in your leap forward is recognizing your independence which can be frightening for some people, especially if they have been in a long-term relationship. Your confidence in the past may have been bolstered by the fact that you were not alone. The fear you may feel comes from anticipating facing the world without a partner. This is where you learn to be brave and discover that being alone is not the end of the world. In fact, being alone can build your inner strength, so that when you do start a relationship, the relationship will be stronger than any you've had before.

Bravery

Before you take any leaps, we need to talk about bravery. Bravery is doing what you need to do, even when you're afraid to do it. If you were the one who initiated the divorce, you might already be familiar with being brave. If you were the reluctant party, you might still need some support in this area.

Often, people stay in relationships because they are afraid. They're afraid of what people may think, or they're scared of being alone. They may be afraid of how the children will handle the divorce. They may be afraid they can't support themselves financially. Some people stay in an unhappy relationship for these reasons. At some point, some of them gather enough bravery to walk out the door and never look back.

Sometimes, it is the person you love who walks out the door. If the relationship is over, then it's over, and there is nothing you can do about it. Bravery here is tricky. It involves a mental and emotional change. You need to be brave enough to let go.

We knew a woman whose husband began treating her poorly. Although they had come into the marriage equally, he started a business and soon began to bring in a load of money. After they had their first child together, he became dismissive of her needs while demanding about his own. She was at home with the baby and had to ask for money for some of the most basic necessities. She could go back to work, but her husband wouldn't help pay for childcare. Her sister told her what to say to bring him into line the next time he was acting out.

The next time he insulted her, she said, "I know you don't think I can make it out there on my own. I want you to know that I can. I don't need you. If you continue to act this way, I'm leaving." This statement changed the balance of their relationship immediately. The husband made a complete turnaround. Today, he's attentive, generous, and kind. Our friend needed to be brave enough to leave her husband to save her marriage.

Whether you decide you're ready for a new relationship or choose to go solo, being brave is your first step in leaping forward. It requires conscious effort and determination. After your divorce, you will need to be brave in situations you never thought about before. You will need to face court, your ex, and the day-to-day aspects of life that your spouse may have handled. No one can do this except you, and *you can* do this!

One man we knew had to face bringing up his three young boys by himself. He remarked, "I need to be brave for my boys." If you have children, you will be able to find bravery for them. It's easier to be brave for someone else than for ourselves. Keep that in mind, and look at yourself from the outside. Can you be brave for *you* as you would be brave for someone else?

Note from Leah...

I believe that bravery is much easier when keeping someone else in mind. If you have kids, think about how brave you are when it comes to protecting them. I get the 'mama-bear' analogy now that I am a mom. It is much easier to channel that energy when doing it for your kids or, even a significant other. But here you are now, and that significant other is not part of the picture anymore. If you are in the process of divorce, then you have already exhibited acts of bravery. Stay strong and keep your head high as you walk through that new door to independence.

Note from Robin...

My first act of bravery happened when I was still married, but close to divorce. I was scared to travel alone with the kids. I was worried about car seats, food, and simply getting on a plane with them. I was worried about traveling by myself. I decided to face my fears of traveling, be brave, and take the kids on vacation by myself.

I called a friend who had moved to another state and asked to visit. She was pleasantly surprised. I booked the tickets and made the arrangements myself. When I got there, I put the kids in a rental car and drove to my friend's house. I knew then that I would be able to make it alone.

Activity: Make a list of your bravest moments. Journal about each one in detail.

<u>Alone is the New Sexy</u>

Before you start a new relationship, you need to be alone. You need time to rediscover yourself. It's only when you know yourself that you can be a part of a healthy relationship. This is a time to "date" yourself. It's time to take yourself to a movie, out to eat, or to some other event – alone.

When you're on your own, you can watch all those movies you never could before. Watching a movie with a partner, like you did in your marriage can be a challenging task. You're different people and may have different tastes in movies. Your ex may not want to watch "comedy," and a comedy may be your all-time favorite movie. A girlfriend once said that she makes any guy she might date watch "The Notebook." It's the first test, she said, to see if they could "emote." If they don't cry, she doesn't date them. You could be into historical dramas, action movies, or foreign films. Your ex could have been into something entirely different. Did you watch what your ex wanted in an effort to please them? Those times are over - you can watch all the movies *you* like!

When you're divorced, funds can be pretty tight. That doesn't mean that you have to stay stuck at home. Once you've caught up with all your favorite movies, it's time to visit friends that you haven't seen for awhile. A lot of times, friends will let you stay at their place so you can save money on a hotel. After all, it *is* just you without the grumpy spouse and loud kids. The world is out there! Explore!

Going out to eat by yourself can be sexy. Think about it. When you're at a restaurant, and you see a person eating alone, what do you think? "Oh! That poor person! Eating by themselves! How *lonely* they must be!" Instead, think about what they're doing there. How do they look? How are they dressed? If they're of the opposite sex, think about how confident they look. Try to catch their eye. Would they like to sit with someone for dinner? Think about how many people would get to know each other if they went out to dinner by themselves!

We recently struck up a conversation with a teenager at a coffee shop. When we asked him what he thought about people dining alone, he gently explained that his generation has an entirely different view of being alone. In his opinion, people of the older generation were stuck staying in unhappy relationships because they feared being alone. He is absolutely comfortable with going to the movies or traveling by himself. There was no stigma attached to being alone.

These are all exercises for your new independence. Every time you carry yourself with confidence, you exude sexiness. Sexy is attractive. Being independent is attractive. You are all of those things. Take yourself out on a date, on a trip, or to a movie. You deserve it.

Note from Leah...

I have a good friend who often travels alone. I admire her bravery. She travels abroad with her itinerary planned and has the greatest stories when she returns. She always meets new people on her solo adventures, and many of the people she meets become her friends for years to come.

On these various trips, she can do whatever she wants. She wakes up and just goes. It may be to a museum, or a play, sitting at a coffee shop all day or finding a street fair. Whatever it may be, she meets more people when traveling alone. She gets better seats at shows and, no matter how packed it is in a bar or restaurant, there is always at least one seat available at the bar.

Furthermore, when she meets others, and they realize she is traveling solo, it is common for them to take her under their wing. I love hearing her stories when she returns from these trips because there is always something fun and exciting that happened.

Note from Robin...

There is a lady who lives nearby. She's in her late 60's, lives alone, and is recently retired. We've struck up a few conversations over the years. Mostly, it's because she's just getting back from some trip. She went to China with a couple of friends, and then she made a trip to Alaska by herself. Her last road trip through the southwest – all by herself.

I want to be like her when I grow up!

I remember going on a trip by myself once in my early 20's, before marriage and children. I took a simple road trip to Sedona and Flagstaff in my little Nissan Sentra. I stayed at a hostel and went on amazing rock climbing adventures and hikes during the day. It was a great vacation because I didn't have to do anything, spend time with anyone (including relatives), and I had nowhere to be at any given time. I also spent little money, aside from the gas, food, and the hostel.

Activity: List the things you never dared to do on your own. Set a date to do them.

<u>Moving</u>

One of the simplest changes you can make in your life, but one that will have big consequences is changing your location. A change in location can be a big or small move. Starting fresh in a new city is a big step and scary, but can help you grow in many ways. If a big move is not available to you, then start small. Move to a new home. It's a fresh start.

We have a friend who did just that. She always wanted to move to California. She lived in Missouri with a man she deeply loved. However, they wanted different things in life. She wanted to move west, and he was content to stay in Missouri forever. She had a hard decision to make. She could remain in Missouri with the man she loved or follow her dreams and move to California. She chose her dreams.

She took the leap and started a new life, and with this new life and location came new friends and experiences. She is an entirely different person today than she was three years ago. She is a stronger woman as a result. She will find love again when the time is right.

Moving allows you to make a lot of changes all at once. If the move is local, you will change the way you drive to work, the stores you shop at, and where you get gas. These small changes will help you take that leap forward with your life because you will discard old ways of doing things. If you make a move to a different city, there are new friends, a new job, and possibly a new culture. This is a bigger change that we recommend you make only after actually thinking it through.

At some point after your divorce, you will need to move. Take your time to decide, but don't wait too long. It's better when you move on your own terms. When you finally move, the change will affect many areas of your life for the better.

Note from Leah...

Once moved into my new home I wanted to change everything, including the decorations, types of furniture, the grocery stores I shopped at, even the streets I took home. These were my decisions, and mine alone, and it felt good. I also realized that initially, I avoided certain restaurants. Why? Oh, right, because my ex didn't like them.

Well, now it's time to go to the places *I* like. I'm creating a new routine as part of my new life. Change feels good.

Note from Robin...

I've had a lot of friends get divorced, and the first physical move sometimes retraces the steps of their last relationship. They get an apartment in the complex where they first met the ex or move back to the city where they first got married. I can tell this is a retrace because they do the same with restaurants, vacations, and other activities. Once the retracing is done, they are ready to move on and go in an entirely different direction.

If you need time to retrace the relationship, take it. You may be working out things in the relationship. When you're ready, you will make the leap into your future and go where you really want to go.

Activity: If you haven't moved, think about when you want to. Explore places that will put you in new social situations.

The Leap to Relationships

The Ideal Partner ~ The Relationship List ~ Marriage

Taking the leap into a new relationship should happen only when *you* are ready. Before you take the leap, think about what it is you want in a relationship. Do you have an ideal partner in mind? Are you really ready to get married again? These are all things to consider when making this leap forward in your life.

The Ideal Partner Starts With You

We all like to think of the Ideal Partner – someone rich, witty, well educated, and good-looking. If you want to be with the Ideal Partner, BE an Ideal Partner first. Get a move on that degree, start that business you always wanted to have, and get to the gym! You *will* attract your Ideal Partner, but you have to be that kind of partner first.

Don't find someone to fix you when you can't fix yourself. Take the time to make sure that you are right with yourself. This is why we emphasize therapy and self-exploration. If you know who you are, you will know what you want.

Your ideal partner might be someone who is financially well off. Are you? Do you have your financial house in order? Do you have a stack of unpaid bills and make rash decisions like going on vacation when your credit card is overdue? If this is the case, why would someone who is financially well-off want to be in a relationship with you?

One of our friends always complained that she couldn't "find" anyone and that all the great guys were taken. Our friend was in a dead end job, dropped out of college, and couldn't seem to keep a roommate. No wonder she couldn't find an Ideal Partner! Another one of our friends gave up on the search for the Ideal Partner and started concentrating on herself. A few years after her divorce, she had a new career and apartment. Suddenly, her Ideal Partner happened!

Take the leap forward in finding your Ideal Partner by starting with you! You may want someone physically fit who goes to the gym and who is active. Have you been doing the same? When thinking of that Ideal Partner, look at yourself first and get yourself together. Use the traits of your Ideal Partner as a road map for achieving that goal. You will find that it's easier to attract the Ideal Partner when you work towards that ideal yourself.

Note from Leah...

It is important to know what an ideal relationship looks like to you. It also helps to write this out. The list is not set in stone, and it will constantly change as you grow in your new life and meet new people but the main points typically stay the same. You will find that you do attract similar minded people. I'm inspired by people I've met who are following their passions and working to better themselves or others. The entire experience has been enlightening. Once you have a clear vision of what you want, you may be amazed at who you attract.

Note from Robin...

I have a problem with hypocrisy. I often hear people complain about finding a quality partner in life, but they spend little time improving themselves. Anyone who takes the time and effort to improve is not going to want to be with a person who can't (or won't) work on themselves.

This hypocrisy goes for both men and women. I see men who don't want to date certain women because they're not pretty enough. I look at the guy and think, "Really? Have *you* looked in the mirror lately?" They're sloppy and out of shape. Work with what nature gave you and make it the best you can.

On the flip side, I see women who won't date men if they don't make enough. Yet, these women are working dead end jobs at low pay, perpetually going to school but never starting a career, or only wishing that a man would come along and rescue them financially. How on earth can a woman expect to be with a man who is financially healthy when she is unable or unwilling to work on her own finances first?

Activity: Make a list with ten things that you want from a relationship. Go ahead! List them out and don't be shy with the details. i.e. *a very muscular man with tattoos. ;P*

<u>The Relationship List</u>

What do you want in a relationship? Did you ever take the time to make a list? If so, did you follow it? It's time to redo that list. You've been through a marriage and learned a lot about relationships (and yourself!) in the process. Now, you have a better idea about what makes you tick and what ticks you off. What can you live with? What can you *not* live without? Put it to paper to help it become a reality.

People will make a list of what they want in a new car, or a house, but never make a list of what they want in a relationship. This list is not to put down the pro's and con's; it's to visualize your relationship at it's best.

There are a lot of things you can put on the list to lay out what your expectations are. For example:

- Trustworthy
- Honest
- Adventurous
- Passionate
- Goal oriented
- Self-reliant
- Sociable

There are also things that are deal-breakers in relationships. These are things you will not compromise on. This is perfectly fine. After all, we do that with cars and homes, right? We have friends who won't buy a home without a garage. Those same friends won't be in a relationship when the other person doesn't have a college degree. Those are their deal breakers.

When choosing a new partner, be discriminating. A new partner is different from just a casual hook-up. This is where you're ready to find "The One" or, at least, "The One" for now. Date, evaluate, discriminate. Don't settle. You don't need to be married to be a person of worth. Instead, find a person who is worthy of you. When in doubt, think, "Would I give up closet space for this person?"

Note from Leah...

I am in a new phase of my life, and I have new wants and needs from a significant other. I look for happy and healthy people. I am a happy person, and I want like-minded individuals. The list you create is evolving. It doesn't have to be filled out completely in one sitting. It will take time. Be particular about what you want. The person you're with should complement you. He or she should make you feel enhanced as a result of spending time together. This person should bring out the light in you. You should not settle for anything less.

Note from Robin...

It was another day, and I was complaining about my ex. My office mate said, "What you did was settle, and now you're pissed off about it" Ouch. How right that was. I married too soon and ended up regretting it. Why is it that we don't recognize our value or worth when it comes to choosing a new partner? Why was it that I was so desperate for marriage that I settled for the first man that seemed to be marriage material, but ended up being headache material? I wish I had taken more time to date a variety of people and learn from those mistakes. Instead, I made a huge mistake and got married, which took a lot longer to get out of, instead of trying to get out of a non-marital relationship.

Activity: Make a two-column list. In the first column, list the full expectations for your next relationship. In the second column, write the deal breakers. Read this list often.

Marriage is not Mandatory

Did you know that not everyone gets married? Yup! It's true! Did you know that unmarried people can be quite happy? Yup! That's true, too! Now that you've been through a marriage and divorce, it's really time to think about whether marriage is right for you. Some people can't be alone, and for whatever warped psychological reason, they *must* be with someone no matter who it is, but you do not have to be that person.

People sometimes choose to remarry for reasons besides simply loving someone. Their religious upbringing, tradition, parent's expectations, and tax purposes are just some of the reasons. Some are worried about what other people will think when introducing a boyfriend or girlfriend when in their 40's or 50's.

Being single has advantages and disadvantages. Marriage is the same way. You may be at a point in your life where you want a long-term relationship but no marriage. You may only want to date. You may be ready to take the plunge or to write off relationships altogether.

You do not have to be married to be happy. More and more people are content with living with someone or living alone. Just remember that marriage is not mandatory. It is not required for happiness. If you do it, do it right. You are not an interest rate that needs to be "locked down."

If you do decide to remarry, let it be for the right reasons. You know yourself better now after being divorced and, hopefully, you've taken some time to re-evaluate your life and the type of person you want to share it with. The right reasons for remarrying are different for everyone. What are yours?

Note from Leah...

We live in a society that views marriage as the natural conclusion to a long-term relationship. We also live in a society that has a 50% divorce rate. I think what was a societal norm is now changing. It is becoming more of a societal norm to have a partner, but not always a marriage. I have friends that are in long-term relationships and never marry -- and it works. They have great relationships. Just because you're in a long-term relationship doesn't mean that you have to get married. Do what feels right to *you* and don't worry about what people think. It is your life. You need to take care of YOU.

Note from Robin...

In my early 20's, I thought I would have to be married to make it. I didn't want to have children on my own, I didn't want to buy a house on my own, and most of all, I didn't want to *be* alone. It took me a long time to ask for a divorce because I was too worried about what other people would think of me. But once I decided to break away, I realized it was pride and vanity that were making me stay. Once I let that go, I realized marriage was not required for my happiness. Staying in an unhappy marriage was not good for me, and being married was *not necessary for me to be happy.*

Epiphanies are awesome.

Activity: Write down five of the *right* reasons for you to remarry.

The Celebration

Independence Day ~ Celebrate with a "Just Divorced" Party ~ Birthday Celebrations

Celebrations are ways to express our joy. We celebrate ends and beginnings. Often, those two go hand in hand. A graduation celebration celebrates the end of schooling and the beginning of a new life. A birthday celebrates the year ahead and the passing of the last. Even New Year's Eve would not be complete without the countdown into the New Year. Your divorce is another reason to celebrate. It is the end of one thing and the beginning of another.

A celebration is when you enlist the support and love of your friends and family. Although you will do that throughout your divorce, there are milestones you will reach where a celebration is to thank those who helped you through it. Take this life event and make it something to celebrate.

Independence Day

There are stages to go through when you separate from your ex. There's the initial separation, the emotional acceptance that it's really over, and the conclusion of the legal process. The initial separation is painful for everyone. It doesn't matter if you were the asking party or the reluctant party; divorce is a time filled with stress and apprehension. Your life will be in flux, and there are a lot of living arrangements to work out.

After a while, and this could be before your divorce is finalized or sometime well after, you will move into acceptance that the relationship is over. *This* is the time to celebrate your independence. An Independence Day Party is just that: a celebration. You have finally realized that it is really over. There is no turning back. An Independence Day Party is a letting go event to show you are ready to move forward in other areas of your life.

One of our friends finally got rid of an ex by moving to a new house without him. We gathered and celebrated with a party in the city. We knew how long it took to finally gain that independence, so many of her friends came to celebrate it!

Your Independence Day Party can be a small at-home gathering or an outing to a restaurant or bar. Use this celebration to thank those who are there for giving their support during your marriage and while you were separating. Speak to each of them. This celebration can offer closure for you at the end of the relationship. After the celebration, you will feel like it's really and truly over. It will make the leap forward easier by commemorating the time when you realized you could move on.

Note from Leah...

The Independence Day may not be just one day. It can be the day you make the decision, move out or file for divorce. The big day is when the divorce is finalized, and this should be celebrated well. We get to that in the next section. There are many reasons to celebrate a significant change in your life with the ones you love and who care for you. Your friends will be there with you. It is where you show them your appreciation and kindness. I have had several Independence Day celebrations. They are a necessity during this process.

Note from Robin...

I have a girlfriend who used to do this in high school whenever someone in her group of friends got over an ex. There was the initial break-up, then a period of complaining, mourning, or anger. Once someone got over that part, it was now a point where they knew they were over their ex. They were ready to move on to another relationship or simply go solo. The rest of the group would get a cake to celebrate the actual conclusion of the old relationship. It was a wonderful way for them to recognize that relationships have many stages. The final stage is acceptance that it's over.

Activity: Arrange an Independence Day celebration with your friends. This could be a dinner out/in, movie night, bar hopping, whatever your heart desires.

Celebrate with a "Just Divorced" Party

A "Just Divorced" Party is the celebration of the conclusion of the legal process of your divorce. The party takes place when the court finalizes the divorce and stamps the legal paperwork, files it, and gives a date for the dissolution of the marriage. Divorces take time to finish. Some take a year, and some take several years. Rarely do we see one that finishes in under a year. Even the friendliest of divorces will have some delays. Completing this process is a great reason to celebrate.

For some of you, a "Just Divorced" Party is an absolute must. You are about to go into a new phase of your life. Embrace it. When organizing your divorce party, complete with a "Just Divorced!" sash if you're a woman, think about registering at an online or local department store. After all, you just split up a household and the ex got some items that you now need to replace. When you send out your invitations, you can include a note: "My ex got all the pots and pans! Help me rebuild my life!"

You may have been over your ex for months or years before your divorce is final, or you may not be over them until years after. Either way, having a celebration at the conclusion of the legal proceedings shows that you reached a milestone. Some of you will have a low-key celebration by meeting with friends at home or out on the town. Even meeting with a friend or two for coffee to share the news is good. It's a chance to let go of self-pity and show appreciation.

An excellent way to bring your friends together is to have a "Just Divorced" Vegas Trip. It will be a memorable one! Have fun people go along for it. No Drama! See a strip show or something comparable... dancing, getting dressed up, and enjoy your new freedom! It has likely been a while since you've cut loose. What better way to kick off your new life than with your friends! Celebrate your freedom!

Note from Leah...

On to the fun stuff! The finalization of a divorce is a big day. It marks the ending of your previous life. It must be celebrated. It is time to get your "Just Divorced" sash and go out on the town. We have done this on several occasions with different friends going through divorce or a breakup. The attention you receive when people read the "Just Divorced" sash is priceless.

It's an event that many people have experienced so you will find that strangers will be congratulating you, high-fiving, even hugging. It is a confidence boost and a good reminder that you're not alone in this process. Over half of marriages end in divorce. Approach it with dignity and strength, and celebrate each milestone with some fun.

Note from Robin...

One of my friends finished a nine-year relationship that culminated with his girlfriend moving out and taking all the Tupperware. My suggestion was to have a "My ex left and took all the Tupperware" party, complete with registry at the local department store.

A divorce doesn't have to be a devastating end. It can be a celebration. Leah and I have a "Just Divorced" sash we now share. We first used it after my divorce was finalized and partied downtown with all of the "Bride to Be" sashes. It was a way to say, "It's over and it's OK!" People laughed when they saw, and we received many rounds of free drinks. The sash was such a hit that we would go out with other friends who were actually married and gave them a turn to wear the sash for fun.

Activity: Plan your 'just divorced' party! First, make a playlist, or find one online. Next, plan the details. Where will you go? How long will it take to get there?

<u>Birthday Celebrations</u>

When you were married, you and your spouse may have arranged birthday celebrations for one another. Sometimes, there's an expectation in marriage that one partner will arrange the birthday celebration of the other. Now it's time to plan your own birthday parties. Don't worry – no one has to know how old you are. You can come up with the age that best suits you! Have some friends over for dinner or do a night on the town. If it's a milestone birthday, plan something big because you're only that age once!

A woman we met always held her birthday with her husband, since their birthdays were within a week of one another. After her divorce, she continued the celebration, which she was always in charge of arranging while she was married. Her ex planned nothing for his birthday and then complained to his friends that no one cared. What did their mutual friends do? They went to our friend's party!

When you get older, birthdays seem less significant. If you have kids, you spend a lot of time planning your children's birthday celebrations and put yours on the back burner. It's important to treat yourself and have at least one great birthday celebration after your divorce. It will help bring your friends and family together, and it's a very good time to socialize and catch up.

If planning your own party is too big of a task, think about partnering with a friend who has a birthday close to yours. You can combine resources, guest lists, and cost. Your mutual friends will be happy to attend only one event instead of a couple.

Note from Leah...

One of my best friends and I have birthdays within days of each other. We have a tradition to plan a shared birthday event each year. The themes change each year. At times we will plan a trip away, or we may stay within town. Either way, we make a point to celebrate, and now it is something we look forward to each year. Now that you don't have to coordinate your schedule with your ex, this is a great new tradition to start.

If you're not good at planning, recruit a friend that is. We all have them. Personally, I love planning events including my own. A time for celebration is a great excuse to get your friends together and plan that trip you've wanted to take. And because it's your birthday it is likely they will arrange their plans to make it work. If it happens to be a milestone birthday, there's even more reason to celebrate.

Note from Robin...

I planned my own 40th birthday party with a huge celebration. After years of disappointing birthdays with the ex, I was ready to take the celebration into my own hands. I booked a table at an exclusive club and invited some special friends to party with me. Years after, we all still talk about that evening. It was worth every penny!

Activity: Plan your next birthday celebration or call your best friend to assist with the planning.

CONCLUSION

Congratulations for so many reasons! You're getting through a divorce, and now you have the tools to help make the journey easier! Following this conclusion, we have listed "101 Things to Do" for practice every day. It's a long list but it encompasses everything you have read. Start at number one and work your way down. If you get through one thing on the list each day, you are a winner!!

Following the "101 Things to Do", we have also listed the activities already read and put them in an "Activities Summary." These are the things to do that require more time. Trying one a day, or even one a week will help make your divorce smoother and your life more manageable. Some of the activities only need to be done once. Others you will return to again and again. However, before you finish this book, we have the one activity that you should try first:

GET
LAID

Yes, we are saying this again. After reading this book, you now have the confidence to get out there and Get Laid! Of course, you also have the confidence to do many other things, but this one is important.

"There are no mistakes, only happy accidents. Everything happens for a reason."

While married, one of us bought a sign that said this and it hung on the kitchen wall. It was a reminder that no matter what happens there is a reason for it. We believe that to this day. Happy accident, or even *not so happy* accident, is how it feels at times. There will be good and bad days throughout this journey. Remember the storms? The storms will rage, but you can always dance in the rain.

You may find yourself going about your day and all the sudden hear a song that was from a happier time in your relationship and find yourself crying. It happens. Let it out. If you're home alone, even more reason to cry it out. You will feel better by letting go of those tears. Those tears are you healing. You may think in these moments of sadness thinking *"the reason why I got married was to have the stability of another person to help me through hard times and yet here I am in a hard time and that person is the cause of it."* These are the kind of emotions you will go through. **You are strong and you will get through this.**

You may go for months, happy to be out of the situation. But the mourning will occur at some point and it may catch you off guard. Every person has their own journey. There will be days that suck, days of pure joy and happiness, and a lot of days in between. Hang in there and power through. It's good to be strong, but it's okay to have your moments of unhappiness too. It's what makes it a charmed divorce. Do it the Charmed Way!

101 Things To Do

The Daily List

1. Get Laid (or do it yourself!).
2. Practice Mindful Breathing.
3. Stretch your body.
4. Get enough sleep.
5. Think positive thoughts.
6. Set a goal for the day.
7. Say "Thank you" to someone.
8. Smile at a stranger.
9. Take the time to look good.
10. Turn off the news.
11. Release negative thoughts.
12. Speak kindly.
13. Ask for help.
14. Break a sweat.
15. Appreciate something in your home.
16. Tidy up.
17. Eat a piece of fruit.
18. Look in the mirror and say, "I Forgive......"
19. Journal.
20. Drink water.
21. Exercise
22. Say, "I will get through this."
23. Be brave.
24. Inhale and exhale.
25. Laugh.
26. Be present in this moment.
27. Listen to an inspirational podcast.
28. Eat something green (not candy!).

29. Let go.
30. Say, "I'm worth it." Out. Loud.
31. Make a list of positive things.
32. Write or re-write your goals.
33. Stay calm.
34. Appreciate something about your work.
35. Listen to music.
36. Express gratitude toward someone.
37. Clean as you go.
38. Dance!
39. Draw something.
40. Call or text a friend.
41. Think of a happy memory.
42. Floss your teeth.
43. Give a compliment.
44. Look in a mirror and say, "I'm hot."
45. Give yourself a time out.
46. Observe someone.
47. Call or text a family member.
48. Find a cluttered place in your home and straighten it.
49. Disengage from a negative person.
50. Contact a business or work connection.
51. Review your resume.
52. Take your vitamins.
53. Learn something new.
54. Do one thing you've been procrastinating on.
55. Delegate a mundane task.
56. Drink a glass of wine.
57. Take a new class.
58. Walk gracefully.
59. Throw away something old (including food!).
60. Say, "You're welcome."

61. Slow down.
62. Sit straight.
63. Hug someone you love.
64. Prepare a healthy meal.
65. Savor the food you eat.
66. Use a timer for tasks at work.
67. Look in a mirror and say, "I'm sexy."
68. Try something new.
69. Question motives.
70. Make a sticky note with a positive affirmation.
71. Meditate.
72. Learn from someone else's mistake.
73. Graciously accept praise.
74. Take five minutes to look at something beautiful.
75. Take a short nature walk.
76. Tilt your head towards the sun and smile.
77. Hold hands with someone.
78. Think before you speak.
79. Save emotional emails for later.
80. If it's raining, dance in it!
81. Buy yourself something (it can be small!).
82. Wear sunscreen.
83. Think of a beautiful part of your body.
84. Smile at yourself in the mirror.
85. Smell something beautiful.
86. Forgive yourself.
87. Choose happiness.
88. Think of a positive influence in your life.
89. Let go of expectations.
90. Daydream.
91. Say to yourself, "I am FREE."
92. Read for enjoyment.

93. Move forward.
94. Work on a travel plan.
95. Wear cute shoes.
96. Organize your desk.
97. Trust your intuition.
98. Make a list of things to do tomorrow.
99. Relax before bed.
100. Before you sleep, say, "I love myself."
101. Get to bed early.

Activities Summary

1	Get laid. Seriously. You know what they say. "That person is cranky! They need to get laid!"
2	Make a list of the top things you want to do for yourself this week. Start marking them off as you treat yourself to as many as you can.
3	List the five top exercises you have heard about that sparked your interest. Look for deals in your area and sign up. Find your favorite. Be excited to try something new. Did someone say pole dancing?
4	Create a bedtime routine or download an app to help you get enough sleep. Sleep is a lot cheaper than a fancy eye cream.
5	Breathe with intent. Inhale deeply for four seconds. Hold your breath for four seconds, and exhale for four seconds. This really works for calming. Practice it. Remember 4-4-4.
6	We challenge you to think about what is bothering you most in this moment. Now, visualize the outcome you would like to see. Try and feel that moment, visualize your surroundings, facial expressions, etc. Practicing this will help. Do this when you are worried or stressed about an upcoming situation. Visualize the positive outcome you desire.
7	Learn to let it go. Close your eyes. Breathe. Let go of all the thoughts racing in your head. Focus on something peaceful. Do this when you need to be fully present.

8	Go online and research therapists in your area or ask friends. Look for people who have experience with divorce. You don't have to call them right now but the information will be there if you need it.
9	On a sheet of paper list four things that are bothering you most in this moment. Now, rip it up in many pieces, and let it go.
10	Create a list of the ten things that pop in your mind that you're truly appreciative of. Wow, look how fortunate you are! Be grateful.
11	Make your personal playlist to uplift your mood and dance to it!
12	Look in the mirror, each day, for 30 days and say, "I am FREE."
13	Make a list of the energy vampires in your life. Put them on a diet.
14	Create a list of the five people closest to you. What type of energy do they display? (i.e. negative, complaining, positive, happy) Now, write a list of the five people in your life that have positive energy. It may be that you have never thought about the type of vibe your tribe is putting off. Knowing is half the battle!
15	Make a list of safe places. They should be places that leave you feeling calm, happy, content and peaceful.
16	Research a support group in your area. It can be divorce related or related to some other issue that you've had in your life. Try one meeting.

17	Make a list of all the things from the past you are holding on to... anger, resentment, or guilt? List them, read them out loud, and then rip up the page and let it go. Free yourself.
18	Create a "Kindness Journal." Write down ways you can show kindness to others.
19	Schedule an activity just for you. Take a nap, bath, walk on the beach or go get your toes done. It's time for a 'Just me' timeout.
20	Schedule a fun activity with your kids. It can be the beach, park, etc. Have a fun day and leave all your anxieties and stressors at home.
21	Take a look at parenting classes in your community. If there's a free one, check it out.
22	Buy a children's book on divorce.
23	When you're ready, send a card or photos to your in-laws. Keep the communication lines open.
24	Make a list of things your ex says. Write the translation out so you follow the feet and not the words.
25	Write a letter to your immediate family, letting them know you appreciate their support.
26	If there's a Future Ex, make a list of kind things to say at the end of each written conversation.
27	Write a list of non-expectations.
28	Write down your ex's name. Next to it write, I am not responsible for his or her happiness.
29	Un-friend the ex.

30	Your relationship broke. It's true. It broke and will not get fixed. Break something. A vase. A plate. A diet. Find something in your house that you can break, or buy something cheap to break. Take a hammer to it. Smash it up. Get the anger out. You will feel better afterwards.
31	Get tested.
32	Start with one drawer and clean it out. Just do one drawer at a time. Before you know it your home will be de-cluttered, and so will your mind.
33	Assess your home and belongings. What is no longer serving you at this phase in your life? It is okay to purge. Have a yard sale or donate. Shed things from your life that no longer serve a purpose.
34	Buy a new soap, scrub or lotion. Try something new!
35	Make a list of things that you have thought about trying but never felt you had the time for. It could be a new type of food, class, or social group.
36	Re-organize your closet. Have all your favorite pieces of clothes easily accessible.
37	Make a list of your top five outfits. Be detailed. Include clothes, shoes, makeup, hair. Now you have your top five outfits ready for future dates. You're welcome!
38	Update the muff.
39	Create a spreadsheet and file folder on your computer and start keeping all your documents in one place. You will be thankful when you need to reference in the future.

40	Download a list of financial and legal things to be done when getting a divorce. Make sure changing beneficiaries is the first. Start saving cash today.
41	Write a list of specific legal questions you need answered. Do some preliminary research. If you do hire an attorney or paralegal, the information you find will help you to ask specific questions to get the answers you need.
42	Make a list of all your electronic devices, including those synched to the cloud. Change the passwords today.
43	Review your to-do list. What can a third party handle?
44	Reach out to that friend or family member who offered to help and take them up on their offer.
45	Check the internet for your next "How-to" project. You just may be amazed on how easy it is to do yourself.
46	Make a date with a friend. You'll come home feeling so much better. Laughter is key.
47	Schedule a dinner with a mix of your couple and single friends.
48	Look up social groups in your area with your top three areas of interests. Sign up for one.
49	Try a new social site for dating or to find new friends. Log in and explore.
50	Practice writing your dating profile page.
51	Write about your dream date. Be detailed. What's the weather like, atmosphere? What music is playing? Have fun with it!

52	Review your dating activities and ensure that your online profiles are private.
53	Make a list of exes and put them on a Do Not Call List.
54	What's on your bucket list? Travel? Languages? Threesomes? Not only should you make a bucket list, you should start checking items off of it as soon as possible.
55	Make a list of your perfect day. Incorporate at least one thing each day. You may find your passion as a result.
56	What did you want to do when you grew up? Is that what you're doing now? What do you want to be doing now? Answer these questions.
57	Write down a business you would like to start. Make detailed plans.
58	Make a list of your favorite meals. Prepare the top three for the week. Viola! You have your lunch and dinner for the week.
59	Find your favorite red or white wines. Check your local Trader Joes, World Market or an online wine club! They are all great sources.
60	Make a travel plan. Enjoy the process of putting it together.
61	Make a list of your bravest moments. Journal about each one in detail.
62	List the things you never dared to do on your own. Set a date to do them.

63	If you haven't moved, think about when you want to. Explore places that will put you in new social situations.
64	Make a list with ten things that you want from a relationship. Go ahead! List them out and don't be shy with the details. i.e. *a very muscular man with tattoos.* ;P
65	Make a two-column list. In the first column, list the absolute expectations for your next relationship. In the second column, write the deal breakers. Read this list often.
66	Write down five of the *right* reasons for you to remarry.
67	Arrange an Independence Day celebration with your friends. This could be a dinner out/in, movie night, bar hopping, whatever your heart desires.
68	Plan your 'just divorced' party! First make a playlist, or find one online. Next, plan the details. Where will you go? How long will it take to get there?
69	Plan your next birthday celebration or call your best friend to assist with the planning.

Printed in the United States
By Bookmasters